Tales of a Toxic Teacher

Exposing the Cycles of Abuse within our Schools

By: Angela Harders

Copyright © 2021 Angela Harders and PAX Publishing

Author, Editor, and Cover Design: Angela Harders
@PeacefulWorldschooler
Artwork, Lettering, and Cover Design: AP Hurtarte @HurtarteStudio

All rights reserved. This book and any portion thereof may not be reproduced or used in any manner whatsoever without the express written permission of the author except for the use of quotations in a book review.

ISBN-13: 978-1-7334285-5-2

To my students,
Each of you have taught me
far more than I could ever
have taught you.

REVIEWS

Tales of a Toxic Teacher explores the many painful and abusive relationships teachers and students have with each other and with the public education system. It is an honest account of how the public education system stifles the innate creativity and curiosity of our children over the course of their time in the system. If we are truly committed to change the current paradigm of public education, a first step would be to read this book to understand the dynamics that must be eradicated. Angela accurately describes each, offering personal examples for a view into your local public school. This book is fantastic!

Brenda M. Diaz
Teacher and Educator
Founder of *The Red Lipstick Rebellion*

We each want to believe that what we do (and especially what we get paid to do) is worthwhile and useful, and that our efforts are making the world a better place. In her book, *Tales of a Toxic Teacher*, former teacher Angela Harders shows the courage and honesty necessary to objectively reconsider and re-examine what she, as part of the American "education" system, has actually contributed to society. Her conclusions do not paint a pretty picture, but it is a picture which we all need to take a long and careful look at if we hope to ever move the world from the way things are to the way things should be.

Larken Rose
Voluntaryist and Author of
The Most Dangerous Superstition

Angela Harders has taken a brave and bold move in writing this book, providing a "fly on the wall" insight into what really happens in schools in some of the richest countries in the world. She has vulnerably and honestly shared her own misgivings, toxic behaviours, and classroom experiences, which so many teachers and former teachers (myself included) can relate to, highlighting how both teachers and students alike become pawns in the toxic environment that permeates our schools. A radical, new approach is needed for education. But for this to happen – and to be successful, not just rhetoric, we must first have an honest look at what is not working and why this is. This book is a much-needed first step to unraveling a thorny and hugely important issue which will have a ripple effect for decades to come. I highly recommend this book!

Clare Ford
Expert Education Coach
Founder & CEO of *Switched ON! Academy*

Table of Contents

INTRODUCTION 8

CHAPTER 1: Power and Control 17

CHAPTER 2: Threats and Coercion 33

CHAPTER 3: Force and Intimidation 45

CHAPTER 4: Emotional Abuse 59

CHAPTER 5: Isolation 83

CHAPTER 6: Minimizing, Denying, and Blaming 99

CHAPTER 7: Using Children 121

CHAPTER 8: Adult Privilege 135

CHAPTER 9: Economic Abuse 149

CHAPTER 10: The Antidote 165

CHAPTER 11: Epilogue 187

SPECIAL THANKS 192

Appendix A: The Power and Control Wheel 194

INTRODUCTION

I am a toxic teacher. I promise I didn't start out this way. The truth is, no teacher ever does. But eventually, we all become one – and most of the time, we never even notice. Teachers do not join the profession to become famous or to make a lot of money. Every single teacher that I have ever known has made the choice to become a teacher because they love children, and they want to make a difference in the world by making a difference in the life of a child (or perhaps thousands of children).

So how do things go so wrong? How does a teacher start a career with the best of intentions to help children and then end up hurting them instead? What is the antidote for a toxic teacher?

INTRODUCTION

Before we dive into the answers to those questions, I wanted to introduce myself to you. My name is Angela Harders. I grew up attending a small private Christian school in the suburbs of Washington, D.C. I had just 31 students in my whole grade, and most of us had been together from Pre-Kindergarten through 8th grade. We not only attended school together during the day, but we also played sports on the same teams after school and on the weekends, and most of us attended the same church (with most of our teachers). School had become an extension of family.

While I did experience some of the "usual" school problems like bullying or gossip, overall, I would say my experience in school was a positive one. I loved my teachers. I loved my friends. I loved learning new things. I loved getting good grades. I loved playing at recess. I loved going on field trips. I loved school – or at least that's what I thought.

Compared to the other schools in my area, my classmates and I lived relatively sheltered lives. We did not worry about skipping class or sneaking around. We did not worry about fights in the hallway or weapons being brought to school. We did not worry about drugs or alcohol. We all really tried to be "good kids."

Even as an 8th grader, I gasped when I heard a student say, "Shut up!" to another student. The worst four letter word that I knew was "crap" or "jerk." So, you can imagine my complete culture shock when my parents transferred me to our local public school – one of the largest in the state – for 9th grade.

TALES OF A TOXIC TEACHER

While I struggled to fit in socially with the two thousand other students, I managed to excel in school and in sports. I was known as a "teacher's pet," made honor roll every semester, took all AP and honors classes, was the starting pitcher for our school's softball team, got an internship at a local elementary school, won several academic and community service awards, and earned multiple scholarships to college.

After high school, I attended Liberty University, the largest Christian university in the world. I worked overtime to graduate with two bachelor's degrees – one in Spanish and one in Teaching English as a Second Language – in just two and half years. I graduated with honors and began to prepare for the next season of my life – more school!

You see, I loved school. And I was good at it. I also loved children. I had spent every summer since 8th grade volunteering in an orphanage in Guatemala, and I knew since then that I wanted to be a teacher and work with kids for the rest of my life.

I truly believed that making a difference in the life of a child is the greatest way to make a difference in the world. I could not imagine investing my time or energy in any lesser endeavor, and so shortly before graduation from college, I applied for an alternative teacher certification program (similar to Teach for America).

Alternative Teacher Certification programs are highly competitive programs in which an outside entity extensively interviews and intensively trains people that have demonstrated

INTRODUCTION

natural teaching ability and then sends them to work in Title I schools in exchange for earning their teacher certification. After several weeks of interviews, writing multiple essays, and performing a "mock lesson" in front of judges, I was pleasantly surprised to learn that I was chosen out of almost five thousand applicants to be one of ten teachers that was accepted to the alternative teacher certification program.

The Monday after my college graduation, I began a two month long intensive training on education theory, pedagogy, lesson planning, formative and summative assessments, scaffolding, small groups, interventions, and more. I spent over 12 hours a day researching and preparing to step foot into my very own classroom, but there would never be enough hours in the day or days in the year to *fully* prepare me for that first day of school.

I was hired to teach Spanish 1 at a Title I school in Prince George's County. On my first day, my supervisor handed me an eraser with no chalk and a stapler with no staples, and said, "Good luck!" She walked me to my classroom, handed me the key, and left. The classroom walls were cinder blocks painted a dull white. There were no windows. The thermostat read 87 degrees. This empty, hot room would be my home for the next year, and I had only a few days to get it ready.

I drove to a nearby teacher store and spent a few hundred dollars on inspirational posters, markers, fancy pens, flags for all the Spanish-speaking countries, red hot chili pepper borders for the bulletin board, stickers, and more. By the end of the day, my empty classroom was starting to look and feel more like home.

I was going to be the best teacher that these kids had ever had!

On the first day of school, I stood at the front door of my classroom with palms drenched in sweat and a grin from ear to ear. I had been warned repeatedly by veteran teachers: "Don't smile until Christmas!" But I just couldn't help myself. I was so excited and so nervous. I had waited and prepared so long for this day – and it was finally here! I was a real teacher about to welcome my real students for the very first time.

The bell rang, and a flood of high school students poured into my classroom. I noticed right away that there was a big problem. I had 30 desks, but my class roster showed 42 students. One student decided that he would take a seat and hang his feet on the desk in front of him. I approached him saying, "Good morning! Can you please move your feet so that someone else can sit here?"

To my utter shock, he stood up towering over me, put his finger in my face and screamed, "Bitch! Who the fuck do you think you are tellin' me what to do? I'll sit wherever the fuck I want!"

"I'm your teacher," I replied praying that my voice wouldn't crack.

"Man, fuck this class, and fuck you!"

INTRODUCTION

He picked up the desk, threw it at me, and walked out of class. I never saw him again – until graduation day when I watched in complete confusion as he walked across the stage and the principal handed him a diploma.

"Hey! How did *he* graduate? He needed to pass Spanish, but he never attended my class," I whispered to my co-worker sitting beside me.

She shook her head. "Don't ask questions. Do you *really* want them to fail him and have him be *our* problem for one more year? Sometimes it's better to just let them through so then they can be society's problem and not ours."

After the graduation ended, I went back to the school and logged onto our online gradebook. I held the printed copy of the grades that I submitted for him – 0% for all four quarters. But the computer was showing something very different. Someone had given him 60% for all four quarters.

He passed my class without ever attending, and he wasn't the only one. He may have passed my class, but we had surely failed him and others like him.

From the first five minutes of my first year teaching, I feared that something was deeply wrong. But by the last five minutes of my first year teaching, I *knew* beyond a shadow of a doubt that something was indeed deeply wrong, and I was a part of the problem.

So many things had transpired that first year and in the following years that made me become a toxic teacher. Many of the stories that you will read in this book are mine, but I will also be sharing stories from other teachers and students. In order to protect the people and places involved, names will be changed, but the truth of our story will not.

You see, everyone knows that there is a problem with the educational system today, but we cannot address a problem as long as we refuse to be honest about it. After all, the first step to recovery is admitting that you have a problem.

While it may be easy and tempting as a teacher to blame the number of other potential causes of problems in the public school:

- Lack of resources
- Lack of parental support
- Lack of administrative support
- Lack of funding
- Lack of student motivation
- Lack of teacher training

I know that it is not helpful for me to address problems that I have no control over. But one thing that I can control is *myself*. I had become a part of the problem, so I *had* to also become a part of the solution. And you can, too!

So, whether you are a Toxic Teacher like me, a parent, a student, or just someone who cares about children, please know that you are not alone, and there is hope. We can solve the problems we cause. We can. We will. We must.

We can solve the problems we cause.

We can.
We will.
~~We must.~~

We Must.

— Angela Harders

CHAPTER 1
Power and Control

Teachers are known for being empaths. We love people. We serve. We care. We sacrifice ourselves for the good of others. We work hard. We go above and beyond. Our job is not merely a job; it's our calling, our mission, our identity, our purpose.

But there is a reason why almost 50% of new teachers leave the profession within the first 5 years. Something is deeply wrong.

How can so many people who love children just seemingly give up on them? How can so many people who want to make a difference in the world just walk away? How can so

TALES OF A TOXIC TEACHER

many people who started a career with hope and excitement leave after a few years with critical and cynical desperation and frustration?

I had read this statistic about teachers leaving within the first 5 years, so I promised myself that I would not just be another statistic. I was going to make it through the first five years – no matter what! And I did.

I taught for 6 years before finally calling it quits. I taught Spanish for 2 years at a high school, English for Speakers of Other Languages (ESOL) for 3 years at an elementary school, and served as the World Language Supervisor for 1 year at a middle school. I had officially taught every grade from Kindergarten through 12th grade, and I was done.

I had taught in schools that had almost all of the student population on Free and Reduced Meals (FARMs), and I had also taught in a school that was located in one of the wealthiest neighborhoods in the area. I taught in a school that was almost entirely African American, one that was a pretty even mix of African American and Hispanic, and one that was more evenly diverse. There were things that I loved and hated about each of the schools that I worked at. But no matter which school I taught at, every single school had problems.

The schools that I worked at in lower income areas had a real problem with not having adequate supplies. One year for Christmas, my parents bought me a box of copy paper and a gift card for Staples because our administration refused to allow teachers to make copies on the copy machines at school. It didn't matter much though because the copy machines were broken more often than they were working.

At the high school, the students didn't have enough textbooks. We barely had enough for a classroom set, and the books were so outdated that they were essentially useless anyway. But again, it didn't matter much because most of the students were not able to read fluently anyway.

I also began to see problems with many of the parents. Most of my students had parents that were divorced, absent, abusive, apathetic, controlling, uninvolved, in prison, in other countries, or dead. I have had parents arrive at parent teacher conferences as high as a kite, but at least they showed up. I have had countless parent teacher conferences where the parents never even bothered to come at all. I have seen parents scream and curse at their children while threatening them, "I'll beat your ass when I get you home!" And then I have had parents scream and curse at *me* as their child's teacher for not letting them turn in an assignment 3 months after the deadline.

As an ESOL teacher, my students' parents had often come from other countries, so they were unable to support their students in their learning due to the language barrier. I ended up teaching an English class for the immigrant parents for free before school so that I could teach the parents strategies for supporting their children even though they could not speak the language well.

TALES OF A TOXIC TEACHER

When I taught in a wealthier area, I had the opposite problem. I had parents that would schedule after-school meetings with me in order to figure out how their child could have a higher A because a 93% was "not good enough." They put so much pressure on their children to be perfect and have straight A's, and I would watch these excelling students struggle with anxiety and depression.

And I have had students with a 0% whose parents never say anything at all. I wonder... do they know? Do they care?

I have had students lie to me, steal from me, yell at me, curse at me, and threaten me. I have seen students do all of these things to other students as well.

I have seen children experience things that I, as an adult, could never even begin to imagine – the death of an older brother in a gang fight, the deportation of a father, the murder of a best friend. I have had students who spent more time in juvenile detention than in school.

I have waited after school with a crying child because mom or dad forgot to pick her up again.

I have hugged a crying student who lost their teddy bear at recess and another who lost their child at Planned Parenthood.

I have cowered in fear behind locked doors of a classroom when we heard the alarm that there was a bomb in our school building. I have tried to calm terrified children as we hid under our desks because there was an active shooter in the neighborhood. I have texted my family "I love you" because I feared that I might not make it home from school this time.

I have had students that could barely read or write – and they were older than me.

I have had students that were attending school for the first time in the United States because they were refugees fleeing from their homes. They constantly arrived exhausted because the nightmares would keep them up at night.

I have witnessed drug deals going down on the playground during recess and had students suspended for having sex in the bathrooms.

I have seen children wear the same clothes day after day. I have kept my closets in my classroom stocked with toothbrushes, toothpaste, deodorant, and a snack for those in need.

I have seen children in the United States that arrive at school hungry, tired, depressed, anxious, bullied, mistreated, and abused. And many times, we send them home the exact same way. The laundry list of problems that I have seen in the public school is greater than any book could contain.

Nevertheless, I worked hard to try to address the problems as best as I could. However, the problems with public school were much bigger than anything that I could handle on my own. Instead, I found myself hungry, tired, depressed, anxious, bullied, mistreated, and abused.

Shortly after my daughter turned one, I decided to quit teaching. It was becoming increasingly difficult for me to be the kind of teacher that I wanted to be and be the kind of mom that I wanted to be. I simply could not leave the problems of school at school.

Teaching consumed me. I was committed to being the best teacher that I could be, but to be a great teacher took way more hours than I was being paid for and way more hours than I was able to invest now that I was a single mom. I spent my evenings calling parents for students that were struggling and my weekends planning fun and engaging lessons and researching the best teaching strategies. I was barely sleeping or eating. I constantly felt like I wasn't doing enough for my students, and I wasn't doing enough for my own daughter.

I knew I had to stop when I ended up having a panic attack at school and an ambulance came to take me to the emergency room because I thought I was having a heart attack. The doctor told me that he sees a number of teachers with anxiety and heart issues resulting from the stress of the job. Who knew that a career that I once loved could possibly kill me?

As a single mother, I knew that I had to prioritize my own mental and physical health for my child, so I said, "Good-bye!" to the classroom and took a job making $12 an hour as a nanny in Georgia, so I could spend the whole day with my one-year-old daughter. Best. Decision. Ever!

I was so thankful for the opportunity to be with my little girl as she was growing up. I began to focus all my time and energy into being the best mom that I could be. I learned about attachment parenting and eventually started practicing gentle parenting as she started to get older (in fact, the first book that I published[1] was about my research and my journey to gentle parenting as a Christian).

Shortly after my daughter turned three, I got married, moved back to Maryland, and decided to get a job in the school system again. I wanted to still be able to make a difference for kids, but I did *not* want to return to the stress of the classroom, so I took a job as a secretary for the main office at the same high school that I graduated from. I was able to catch a glimpse of the many things that happen "behind the scenes" at a public school because I worked closely with the administrators. I was quite content to still be able to connect with children but without having to "take work home" like I did when I was a teacher. I could "leave work at work" and be present with my daughter and my husband when I was home.

After one year, I was promoted to the School Financial Specialist (SFS) position. I was responsible for all of the funds related to the school. I wrote all the checks, balanced all the budgets, managed all the grants, helped organize all the field trips and fundraisers, and observed where all the funds went. (I'll be sharing more on school finances in a later chapter). I began to realize that every single school is a business, and every single

---

[1] Harders, Angela. *Gospel-Based Parenting: A Biblical Study on Discipline and Discipling*. 2019. Available for purchase on Amazon or at www.peacefulworldschoolers.com/Gospel-Based-Parenting

student in it is a commodity with a very high price tag attached to every single head. I continued to pull back the layers of corruption within the system – both immoral and illegal.

The whole system is toxic – from the top down and the bottom up. It's no wonder that a toxic system eventually produces toxic results in students *and* staff. The problem with our educational system is deeper and more pervasive than anyone could ever imagine because the problem is *not* that the educational system is broken; the problem is that the educational system is doing exactly what it was designed to do.

Compulsory schooling is a relatively new social experiment that began in Massachusetts around 1850. Schools were designed in large part by a man named Horace Mann after he had observed the Prussian system which was used primarily to indoctrinate the youth with the values that benefited the government and often ran contrary to religious or familial values. In the wake of the Industrial Revolution, Horace Mann saw compulsory schooling as a way to manufacture workers for the factories – workers that would be submissive and subordinate.[2]

In April 1924, H.L. Mencken wrote in *The American Mercury*, the aim of public education is not "to fill the young of

---

[2] While I would love to take you on an in-depth journey through the history of public education, there are others who have already done extensive research on the subject, so rather than add to the brilliant words already spoken and written, I would encourage you to pursue their works. I highly recommend reading The Underground History of American Education by John Taylor Gatto. A free PDF of his book is available on www.peacefulworldschoolers.com/downloads.

the species with knowledge and awaken their intelligence... Nothing could be further from the truth. The aim... is simply to reduce as many individuals as possible to the same safe level, to breed and train a standardized citizenry, to put down dissents and originality. That is its aim in the United States... and that is its aim everywhere else."

American educator, Neil Postman, wrote, "Public education does not serve a public. It *creates* a public. And in creating the right kind of public, the schools contribute toward strengthening the spiritual basis of the American Creed. That is how Jefferson understood it, how Horace Mann understood it, how John Dewey understood it, and in fact, there is no other way to understand it. The question is not, 'Does or doesn't public schooling create a public?' The question is, 'What kind of public does it create?'"

New York City Teacher of the Year and author, John Taylor Gatto, wrote in his best-seller <u>Dumbing Us Down</u>, "The truth is that schools don't really teach anything except how to obey orders. This is a great mystery to me because thousands of humane, caring people work in schools as teachers and aides and administrators, but the abstract logic of the institution overwhelms their individual contributions. Although teachers do care and do work very, very hard, the institution is psychopathic – it has no conscience. It rings a bell, and the young man in the middle of writing a poem must close his notebook and move to a different cell where he must memorize that humans and monkeys derive from a common ancestor."

Noam Chomsky succinctly wrote in <u>Manufacturing Consent,</u> "Education is a system of imposed ignorance."

At the same time that I began to learn more about the dark history of public school, I also began researching another topic that was impacting my life at the time – abuse. My relationship with my husband grew increasingly abusive shortly after our marriage. I assumed that I was just dealing with "normal newlywed problems," but a dear friend of mine encouraged me to research about toxic relationships. That was when I first learned about the Power and Control Wheel.[3]

The Domestic Abuse Intervention Project (DIAP) created the "Power and Control Wheel" in order to help people understand the overall pattern of abusive and violent behaviors that are used to establish and maintain power and control over another person.

---

[3] http://www.ncdsv.org/images/PowerControlwheelNOSHADING.pdf

The Power and Control Wheel Of Domestic Violence

POWER AND CONTROL WHEEL

VIOLENCE — PHYSICAL • SEXUAL

USING COERCION AND THREATS
Making and/or carrying out threats to do something to hurt her • threatening to leave her, to commit suicide, to report her to welfare • making her drop charges • making her do illegal things.

USING INTIMIDATION
Making her afraid by using looks, actions, gestures • smashing things • destroying her property • abusing pets • displaying weapons.

USING EMOTIONAL ABUSE
Putting her down • making her feel bad about herself • calling her names • making her think she's crazy • playing mind games • humiliating her • making her feel guilty.

USING ECONOMIC ABUSE
Preventing her from getting or keeping a job • making her ask for money • giving her an allowance • taking her money • not letting her know about or have access to family income.

USING MALE PRIVILEGE
Treating her like a servant • making all the big decisions • acting like the "master of the castle" • being the one to define men's and women's roles.

USING ISOLATION
Controlling what she does, who she sees and talks to, what she reads, where she goes • limiting her outside involvement • using jealousy to justify actions.

USING CHILDREN
Making her feel guilty about the children • using the children to relay messages • using visitation to harass her • threatening to take the children away.

MINIMIZING, DENYING AND BLAMING
Making light of the abuse and not taking her concerns about it seriously • saying the abuse didn't happen • shifting responsibility for abusive behavior • saying she caused it.

POWER AND CONTROL

VIOLENCE — PHYSICAL • SEXUAL

After reading the wheel and seeing its application in my personal life, I began to also see similar patterns of abuse and violence in my professional life. I decided to create my own Power and Control Wheel showing the ways that toxic teachers in a toxic system produce toxic behaviors that harm children.

The Power and Control Wheel
For Toxic Teachers

Violence — Physical, Sexual, Emotional, Emotional, Physical, Sexual, Violence

Power and Control (center)

Using Coercion and Threats
- Making and/or carrying out threats or punishment
- threatening loss of freedom
- threatening authority involvement/prison
- threatening fines
- manipulating
- bribing

Using Force and Intimidation
- Making children afraid by using mean looks, actions, gestures
- Smashing or throwing things
- Standing over children
- Yelling and screaming
- Confiscating things
- Forcing to do useless tasks
- Silencing

Using Emotional Abuse
- Humiliating children
- Making them feel like failures
- Withholding love and compassion
- Publicly shaming and embarrasing them
- Stonewalling or ignoring the student
- Making fun of a student/name calling

Using Isolation
- Controlling what they do, where they go, who they talk to, what they read, etc.
- Isolating from family, friends, the community or the rest of class
- Putting students in "time out" or detention
- Taking away recess or lunch

Denying, Minimizing, and Blaming
- Making light of abuse
- Blaming the students
- Not taking concerns seriously
- Denying the abuse is happening
- Shifting responsibility for abusive behaviors
- Gaslighting a students' experience

Using Children
- feeling in control
- using children for power
- using children to do tasks
- feeling better about yourself
- threatening to take children away
- using children to communicate with parents or others

Using Adult Privilege
- Treating children like servants or "lesser"
- Enforcing but not following the rules
- Preventing meaningful participation
- Denying rights and privileges
- Making all of the decisions
- Always being "right"
- Inflicting pain
- Bossing

Using Economic Abuse
- Preventing students from getting or keeping a job
- Controlling financial decisions
- Stealing or destroying their belongings
- Withholding access to money that belongs to the students

I remember the very first day that I realized that I had power and control as a teacher that I did not have before. The first day of class, I told my students that for homework, they needed to have their parents sign the class syllabus and return it to me the following day. When they returned the next day, I was a bit surprised that they actually did it!

I called my best friend on my lunch break and told her how strange it was for me that my students just did what I said – just because I said it. They did not know me. They did not know why I was asking for a parent signature. They could have totally forged the signatures, and I would have never known. They did not know what I would do with this paper or any of their other homework or classwork assignments (most of which ended up in the trash can). And yet, they did it. They obeyed. They obeyed without question.

There was no other area of my life where I could just tell a stranger to do something and expect them to just do it simply because I said so. But even recognizing that I had some unique power as a teacher that I did not have before, I still assumed that I could and would use that power and control for good. It did not take me long to realize how totally out of control I really was.

Schools were created to subjugate. Is it any wonder that our classes are called "subjects"? They were designed to implement social hierarchy. Is it any wonder that juniors and seniors in high school are called "upper classmen"?

TALES OF A TOXIC TEACHER

We take children, young, passionate, and curious. We assign them an identification number. We sort them in various levels based on their age. We lock them in a room for 6-8 hours a day. We tell them when they can stand up, sit down, eat, go to the bathroom, and sleep. We assign them various (mostly irrelevant) tasks. We exert power and control. And we expect obedience without question and compliance without resistance.

Abuse cannot exist without power and control. This is precisely why we find power and control at the center of our wheel of abuse. Over the next several chapters, we will explore the various ways that power and control show up in the school system.

I will warn that what I am about to share may shock and disturb you. In fact, I hope that it will. I hope that you will be so disturbed and enraged at the abuse that we have not only permitted but ordained that you will be willing to take the necessary actions to save yourselves and your children. The future of the world depends on it. It depends on *you*.

Power does not corrupt. Fear corrupts... perhaps the fear of losing control.

— John Steinbeck

CHAPTER 2

Threats and Coercion

The entire educational system can only function through threats and coercion. Whether I like to admit it or not, I too am guilty of threatening my students. And if you think that you are innocent of throwing out the occasional threat, then pay attention for some of the following "if, then statements."

"If you don't listen to me, then I'm going to call your parents!"
"If you don't put your phone away, then I will take it from you."
"If you don't pass, then you will fail and repeat the whole year."
"If you don't do your homework, then you'll do it during lunch."

TALES OF A TOXIC TEACHER

"If you don't stop talking, then I'll put you in the Quiet Corner!"
"If you get up, then I'll make you stand for the rest of class."
"If you won't stop playing around, then you'll have no recess!"
"If you don't finish your lunch, then it's going in the trash."
"If you won't take off your hat, then I'm calling security."
"If you don't come to class, then we will notify the police."
"If you talk to me like that, I'll write you up for insubordination."
"If you don't get a C, then you can't play in the game tonight."
"If you don't change your clothes, then you'll be suspended."
"If you don't shut up, then we'll sit in silence until the bell!"
"If you don't behave, then I'm writing your name on the board."
"If you don't stay in line, then you'll go to the principal."
"If you don't raise your hand to speak, then I will ignore you."
"If you don't do exactly what I say, then I will punish you."
"If you don't graduate, then you will be a failure."

    Teachers use threats all the time; although, we may try to refer to them as "consequences" or "external motivation." However, the impact is the same. If a student refuses to obey a teacher's command, then we will usually employ some sort of threat in order to coerce their obedience.

    Coercion is defined as "the practice of persuading someone to do something by using force or threats." From the tender age of five years old, we force a child to leave his family and his home. We place him in a room with one or two adult strangers and 15-30 smaller strangers that are all the same age who were also forced to be there. We force them to repeat, memorize, sing, dance, talk, shut up, stand up, sit down, read, write, count, color, cut, paste, and more. We do not care if they are willing or able to do what we are asking them to do. And if they are not willing or able to do what we are asking them to do, then we threaten them with various types of punishment. All the while touting the phrase that "learning should be fun!" If we want to inspire children to love learning, then we cannot continue to threaten or coerce them into doing so.

When I turned six years old, my parents forced me to take piano lessons. I absolutely hated to practice 15 minutes every day and had no desire to play the kinds of songs that my teacher enjoyed and mistakenly assumed that I should enjoy too.

My parents would threaten me, "If you don't practice piano, then you won't get dessert." When threats wouldn't work, they would result to bribes. "If you practice piano, then I will let you watch a movie after dinner." Coercion turned something beautiful and enjoyable like music into something that was a chore and a bore. I continued to suffer year after year, and the topic became so contentious that it was negatively impacting my relationship with my parents. It seemed as though all we did was fight about playing the piano.

When I turned 13 years old, my parents agreed to stop forcing me, and so I quit taking piano lessons. Much to their surprise, once they stopped forcing me to practice or go to formal lessons, I actually started to grow an interest in playing the piano.

TALES OF A TOXIC TEACHER

I discovered songs that I wanted to learn how to play and spent hours each day trying to master each one.

Playing the piano was still a challenge for me, but it was a challenge that I *chose* – not one that was being forced upon me. I even chose to take piano classes in college, played piano for our church's worship team, and I even teach piano lessons to other children and adults to this day.

Force completely removes the fun from learning. The exact same thing happens in public school on a daily basis. We force children to learn topics that they have absolutely zero interest in and absolutely zero practical use for at that stage in their lives. We force them to study random topics that some curriculum designer thinks that they should learn about, and then we threaten them for not being interested or able to learn that topic or skill yet. We force them to occupy their time and energy with meaningless tasks and threaten to punish them if they fail to comply.

As someone who has taught every grade from kindergarten through 12th grade, I will say that it has been one of the most depressing and heart wrenching experiences for me to observe my students as they make their way through the public school system.

I was the first person to greet Raquel as she entered school for the first time. I can remember how she poked her head out from behind her mother's dress. Her eyes darted around the room as she tried to take it all in.

I got down on one knee, made sure to flash her a big, bright smile and, with my best teacher voice, I said, "Good morning! I'm so glad you're here! We are going to have so much fun! What's your name?"

Her big brown eyes looked up at me in utter fear. She bit her lower lip, and her knuckles turned white as she clenched her mother's dress even tighter. "Raquel," answered her mother. "Se llama Raquel."

I gently reached out my hand, and she took it. I helped remove Raquel's backpack that weighed more than she did and showed her which desk would be her special place for the rest of the year. Her mother waved goodbye, and little Raquel's eyes filled with tears.

After a few weeks, Raquel would run into my classroom, leaving her mother walking briskly behind her, throwing her arms around me for a big hug. "What will we learn about today, Miss Harders?"

It did not matter if we were learning about the colors, the numbers, the letters, or animals, Raquel was excited about it all. In fact, most of my students were. At five years old, the entire world was a mystery, a game, an adventure, and everything about the world was fascinating and exciting.

Raquel loved to learn, but she struggled to keep up with her peers when it came to reading. She loved to draw and paint and color, but by 1st grade, we had labeled her as a "slow learner," and she was placed in the remedial class.

TALES OF A TOXIC TEACHER

I would often stop by to see how she was doing, but instead of the happy, bright girl I knew in Kindergarten, she had become quiet and isolated. The teacher had to follow the curriculum, and unfortunately, Raquel would be left behind.

By 6th grade, Raquel's confidence was completely gone, and apathy was setting in. She was failing all of her classes, but even worse – she believed that *she* was a failure. She refused to do any of her assignments, and she no longer responded to threats by teachers to call her parents.

What was the point?

She was "behind." Behind what?

She was "slow." According to whom?

She was "a lost cause." But *we* created the environment for her to feel that way.

Imagine for a moment that there were no grades, no standardized tests, no quizzes, no homework, nothing to fail, and everything to learn. Imagine for a moment that there was no curriculum designed by politicians or adults so far removed from children or the classroom. Imagine for a moment that each individual unique child had the freedom to pursue his or her own unique passions and interests – completely free from threats and coercion.

Imagine the possibilities that would open up if children were truly free to learn what and when and how they desired. What beautiful things they would create! But instead, we choose threats and coercion.

THREATS AND COERCION

Threats and coercion find their place on the Power and Control Wheel of Abuse because threats and coercion are violence against free human beings – even the tiniest of humans. Mahatma Gandhi once said that "one who uses coercion is guilty of deliberate violence. Coercion is inhuman."

Coercion is violence because it kills. It kills creativity and curiosity. It kills compassion and connection. It kills cooperation and collaboration. And while few people would ever want to admit that they were using coercion – especially against a child – it is important for us to acknowledge and admit that we have, and we do.

As a teacher and as a parent, we all have used threats and coercion against the children in our care. But how can we know if we are using threats or coercion in our interactions with children? Ask yourself:

- Am I making and/or carrying out threats or punishment?
- Am I threatening loss of freedom?
- Am I threatening authority involvement or prison?
- Am I threatening fines or financial consequences?
- Am I manipulating?
- Am I bribing?

Pay attention to any time that you use an if-then statement like I mentioned in the beginning of this chapter. Look for the ways that you utilize punishment. As teachers, we often threaten and coerce children with punishment. Whether it is detention or a D on the top of your paper, we punish. All forms of punishment are detrimental to children, and they are detrimental to our relationship with children.

We threaten children with the loss of freedom. If they do not do everything that we want them to do, they will lose recess time or lunch time. They will lose the opportunity to participate in activities with the group. They will not be permitted to speak to their friends.

But we do not only threaten "bad children" with the loss of freedom. All children in school are devoid of individual basic God-given freedoms and rights. In public school, there is no freedom of speech. There is no freedom of religion. There is no freedom to petition or file a redress against authority. There is no freedom of assembly. There is no freedom of movement. There is no freedom of privacy. There is no freedom from unreasonable search and seizure. And now, in some cases, there is no freedom to even breathe. There is no freedom. Every child in every school is indeed a slave. We merely allow them the "freedom" to choose if they wish to be a "good slave" or a "bad slave," but a slave they will always be.

And if we, as Toxic Teachers, have the misfortune of being stuck with a "bad slave" in our classroom, then we continue to threaten to call a parent, or the principal, or the security guard, or even the police when they don't do what we want.

THREATS AND COERCION

While most people would readily admit that threats and coercion are evil and harmful, there is yet another form of coercion that most people actually believe to be good – the bribe. We attempt to coerce our students into getting good grades by bribing them with meaningless letters, pointless pieces of paper, and absurd accolades. We attempt to coerce our students into "behaving well" (which is simply code for "blind obedience") by bribing them with toys and trinkets and stickers and candy. Perhaps we will dish out some extra credit, bonus points, or a few minutes of extra fun on the playground. Heaven forbid that we actually assume that a human being might freely choose to make a moral decision on their own.

Coercion is not only inhuman and immoral, but it is also illegal. Black's Law Dictionary defines "duress" as "any unlawful threat or *coercion* used… to induce another to act [or refrain from acting] in a manner [they] otherwise would not [or would.]" Most states have criminal charges for coercion and allow for civil action to be taken by district attorneys or the Attorney General. However, few are willing to stand against the coercive practices of a toxic teacher in a toxic system that are being enforced upon our children.

ONE WHO USES COERCION IS GUILTY OF ~~THE~~ VIOLENCE.

COERCION IS INHUMAN.

— Mahatma Gandhi

CHAPTER 3
Force and Intimidation

The "teacher look." I had spent years perfecting it. You know the one. A "good" teacher has the magical power of silencing a room full of rowdy and rambunctious children with just one look. Pursed lips. Glaring eyes staring through your glasses halfway down your nose. A hand on the hip. A foot frantically tapping. The "teacher look" is one of the many tools that I learned how to use in order to maintain power and control over the children in my classroom.

But now, I'm going to let you in on another little secret. In the middle of my first year of teaching, a veteran teacher

TALES OF A TOXIC TEACHER

decided to share this teacher tip with me, and now I will share it with you. There is one tool that transformed my ability to maintain power and control of my classroom – the clipboard.

"If you are struggling with classroom management, the only thing that you need is a clipboard and a pen," she said with a smirk. I learned that it doesn't even matter what you write on that clipboard, but the mere presence of a clipboard and a pen will intimidate any wayward student into correcting their behavior almost immediately. When combined with the "teacher look," the clipboard became one of the most powerful tools that I had in my arsenal.

I remember that one day my class was particularly "enthusiastic." Apparently, there was a fight that had happened that morning and so completing the Spanish warm up for the day was the furthest thing from my students' minds. After asking politely many times for them to be quiet and do their work, I knew that it was time to use the clipboard.

I grabbed the clipboard from my desk, stood in the front of the classroom with my best "teacher look," and I began to write with the dreaded red pen. I slowly drew the words, "I freaking hate this" in the middle of my paper. Then I proceeded to decorate my paper with lovely red hearts and smiley faces. Occasionally, I would look up from the clipboard, lock eyes with a chatty kid, and then proceed to angrily draw more red hearts or a really big smiley face on my clipboard.

FORCE AND INTIMIDATION

I wanted them to think that I was writing down the names of the rebellious or the troublemakers. I tried my best to give the most intimidating of glares as they began to quiet themselves down one by one. When the room was silent, I allowed the suspense and fear to hang in the air for a moment longer. I clutched the clipboard close to my chest so that they would not see my artwork.

After a long silence, I sternly yet calmly announced, "Pull out your notebooks and begin working on your warmup... now." All 38 of them immediately obeyed. My intimidation game had worked again.

Upon hearing the bell ring, I dismissed my class with a smile and then crumpled up the paper from the clipboard, throwing it casually into the trash can without them noticing and before the next group of students would enter for fear that they would learn my teacher secret.

I learned early on in my teaching career that using force and intimidation would be another crucial element in maintaining power and control. While many teachers may use covert methods of intimidation such as the clipboard or the "teacher look," I noticed that some other teachers or administrators prefer to use more overt methods of intimidation such as yelling and screaming.

During my planning period, I would often try to go for a walk throughout the high school to get some exercise and to clear my mind. I could hear other teachers screaming at the top of their

TALES OF A TOXIC TEACHER

lungs, "SIT DOWN AND SHUT UP!" Occasionally, I would even hear a teacher hurling expletives at a student or even at their entire class.

In fact, I must confess that the first time in my life that I ever cursed was in my classroom. I had had enough, and so I did something that I had sworn I would never do.

A co-worker of mine was absent from school because a female student beat the tar out of her the day before, breaking several of her ribs and cracking her skull. What inspired such an outburst of rage in this young girl? The teacher had stretched her arm in front of the building door and told this teenage girl that she was not permitted to leave the school building while class was in session. Naturally, the only rational response to being told that you must stay in school when you're supposed to be in school is that you physically assault someone. And instead of helping the teacher who was being brutally attacked, a large crowd of excited teenagers gathered to film the interaction and quickly post it to social media.

The following day, everyone was talking about what had happened between the girl and the teacher while I was trying to talk about Spanish verb conjugations. Once again, I found myself waiting with my "teacher look" and my clipboard for my students to be quiet long enough for me to give them instructions. I waited 5 minutes... 10 minutes... 15 minutes... and finally I had enough.

I screamed at the top of my lungs, "I AM SICK OF YOU ALL TREATING TEACHERS LIKE SHIT!"

They all knew me as "the nice teacher," so as soon as I screamed at them, they immediately stopped what they were doing and turned to stare at me.

When they were quiet, I continued, "I AM SICK OF SPENDING HOURS AND DAYS OF MY LIFE PLANNING FUN LESSONS FOR YOU WHEN YOU DON'T GIVE A SHIT!" A girl in the front row muttered, "I'm sorry, Miss Harders."

"IF YOU DON'T CARE TO LEARN, THEN WHY SHOULD I CARE TO TEACH?!" I watched as my entire classroom full of young people hung their heads in shame. I knew that I had done and said enough, so I took a deep breath. They got my point.

"I'm done for today. You can work on Spanish, you can work on math, you can work on whatever you want, but I'm done." I walked over to my desk, sat down in my large teacher chair, put the clipboard in the top drawer next to me, slammed the drawer shut, folded my arms, and did not move for the rest of the period.

My students also sat down and began working in complete silence. Some teachers would call that a "win," but for me, it was an epic loss. This was the first day that I realized that I was a Toxic Teacher. I treated these students in a way that I had never treated any other human being before in my life. It was my turn to feel shame.

I was mortified that I had screamed and cursed at them, so the following day I began my class with a deep and sincere apology. "I need to apologize to each of you for the way that I spoke to you yesterday. I was so wrong, and it does not matter what you do or don't do. You do not deserve for anyone else to yell or scream or curse at you. I promised to treat you all with respect and dignity, and yesterday, I failed to do that. I am so so so sorry." Tears started streaming down my cheeks, and several of my students got up from their desks to hug me.

"Miss Harders, *every* teacher yells at us."

"Yeah, don't worry, Miss H. We hear worse at school *and* at home."

"It's all good, Miss Harders. You ain't the first to curse at us, and you won't be the last. We know you really love us."

Their words did not help. The damage was done. I had become a monster, unrecognizable to myself. I had treated these children in such a terrible way that was the opposite of the kind of person that I wanted to be. But even worse, I realized that these children had grown accustomed to being verbally abused and assaulted both in school and at home.

The young girl's physical assault of the teacher the day before was just as damaging as the verbal assaults that my students were experiencing in school and at home. However, we

FORCE AND INTIMIDATION

have been indoctrinated to believe that it is only physical assaults that leave wounds and scars.

After two years teaching Spanish at the high school, I began teaching English at a local elementary school. While the environment was much more positive overall, the children there could not escape intimidation either.

I watched in horror and embarrassment as my colleague stood towering over a disobedient student. Standing over children is one way that Toxic Teachers use intimidation in order to exert their power and control over children.

"Give me the crayon – NOW!" I noticed that she had mastered the "teacher look" too.

The little boy reluctantly held his hand up with the blue crayon poking out of the side. You see, this Toxic Teacher had determined that it was only appropriate to write the vocabulary words of the day with a pencil and not in the boy's favorite color. Why?

"You may get it back at the end of the day if you behave."

Confiscating things is one tactic used by Toxic Teachers. It does not matter if it's a crayon or a cell phone, Toxic Teachers abuse children by exerting their power and control by taking their belongings and holding them as collateral.

We attempt to manipulate and force children to do what we want by intimidating them and threatening to take their belongings. What becomes the difference then between the Toxic Teacher demanding a child's crayon, and the thug on the street demanding your purse? Does a teacher possess some special right or authority to steal someone else's prized possessions? And yet this evil practice happens all over the world on a daily basis.

Another evil practice that happens in every single classroom is the use of force. All day every day teachers force students to do things that they do not want to do. Don't believe me? Just step foot inside a high school math class.

Over the years, I have grown to become increasingly aware of the fact that schools only function through force. And if someone is forced, then they are not free. And so much of what we force children to do is absolutely useless.

Why do we force a five-year-old to identify the difference between a dime and a penny? Why do we force a fifteen-year-old to determine the length of the hypotenuse of a triangle? Why do we force a 9th grader to write an essay about sublimation? Or force a 3rd grader to write a paragraph about the phases of the moon? Why do we force an 8th grader to give a presentation about international trade in the Indian Ocean in 600 CE? Or force a 6th grader to do a group project about leprechauns? Who determines what children need to know and when and how and why?

I cannot help but wonder what would become of the children that are trapped in our classrooms if they were given the gift of freedom instead of force. One night as I pondered that question, I began to write some more in my journal:

FORCE AND INTIMIDATION

What grand things would they discover?
What great questions would they ponder?
What mysteries would they uncover?
What can stop those who wonder
Who? What? When? Where? Why?
Surely, not I.

Schools function through force and intimidation because those in authority need to control the slaves within the system. Children who are compliant and obedient will one day be citizens who will be compliant and obedient. Children who cannot conform to "societal norms" will be labeled as "bad" or "troublemakers" or "special needs."

Toxic Teachers work hard to squash any sort of dissent or individuality by becoming masters of force and control under the guise of "classroom management." We are even trained to control students by pretending to give them choices. For example, a teacher may tell students that they can choose their partner for a project, or which center they want to go to first, or if they want to do a live presentation or a video recording. But these choices are not authentic. The students are still slaves to the curriculum – to someone else's agenda.

By forcing students to do useless or meaningless tasks, we are not testing their intellect, but rather their ability to comply without question. In this way, we demolish critical thinking as well as individualism because the children must blindly comply "for the good of the group."

Count the number of ducks on the page.

Paste some cotton balls in the shape of a C.

Color between the lines.

In fact, we will even tell you which colors you are allowed to use based on a random number system.

Read this book – not that one.

Divide these fractions.

Solve for x.

Balance the equation.

Write the theme.

What happens next?

We teach children to make predictions, but have we taken the time to predict the result of our actions as Toxic Teachers within a toxic system? What will the impact be of attempting to force children to learn things that they could care less about and have no actual relevance or significance in their real life?

Schools can never meet the needs of an individual child because all of our time and effort is spent teaching to a standard. It is impossible to achieve diversity of thought or idea if we are striving for a standard. The arbitrary curriculum drives us forward, and it does not matter who gets left behind. Nevertheless, we teach to the standards. But who determined the standards? Who says that in order to be considered an "educated" human being you must be able to graph the inverse of a function?

Who says that success looks like getting good grades? Never mind if you know how to be a good friend. Who says that learning must be forced upon human beings that are meant to be free? And what a beautiful world would open up if we let them be… free?

I had all these questions looming in my mind, but I never said a thing, because I too was a slave of the toxic system, and I had learned my lessons well. I learned to be silent – to be silenced. Asking questions would pose a threat to the very foundation of the schooling system, so I decided to keep my questions to myself for a time. Just as I, as a teacher, expected blind obedience from my students, my administration expected blind obedience from me.

So, like a faithful slave, I passed along the lessons that I had learned. I would teach my students to be silent. You must raise your hand to speak, and only I had the power to grant them the freedom to open their mouths and say what was on their mind. In fact, we were so obsessed with silencing our students that we would turn it into a game called "The Silent Game." Whoever could stay the quietest the longest would win. I cannot help but wonder if we are still playing this silly game today.

All the teachers who know the truth about the damage being done in schools, we are all playing one massive "Silent Game." Whoever can stay the quietest the longest will win a nice prize called "retirement." But I was never too good at the "Silent Game," as I'm sure you can tell.

TALES OF A TOXIC TEACHER

There's a reason why our Founding Fathers put "freedom of speech" first. They understood the abuse that occurs when individuals or groups are silenced. They understood the power of speech to spark change in tyrannical systems. I suppose you could say this book is my attempt to tap out of the "Silent Game." I hope many others will tap out too.

FORCE COMPLETELY REMOVES THE FUN FROM LEARNING.

— ANGELA HARDERS

CHAPTER 4
Emotional Abuse

I am a little embarrassed to admit that, for most of my life, I did not believe that emotional abuse was real. I assumed that emotional abuse was a lame excuse for wimpy, weak women to complain about their spouses. It wasn't until I experienced the pain and the trauma of emotional abuse within my own marriage that I began to realize how real – and how damaging – emotional abuse can be.

As I learned more about emotional abuse, I started to see parallels between the abuse that was happening in my home and the abuse that was happening in my school. There have not been

TALES OF A TOXIC TEACHER

many studies conducted on emotional abuse in the classroom, but I can assure you that it is one of the most pervasive and destructive forms of abuse today. And just as I was facing emotional abuse both at home and in school, students all over the world are also facing emotional abuse both at home and in school. I bet you did, too.

There are six main types of emotionally abusive behaviors:

- Demeaning/Humiliating
- Discriminating/Biased
- Dominating/Controlling
- Destabilizing/Intimidating
- Distancing/Emotionally Unsupportive
- Diverse/Attitudes that have a negative impact on class climate[4]

DEMEANING

The first example of emotional abuse is **demeaning** or humiliating behavior. I began to reflect on some of the practices that I had done in my classroom or that I had seen in other people's classrooms that I knew had been demeaning and humiliating to students – whether intentionally or unintentionally.

---

[4] McEachern, Adriana & Aluede, Oyaziwo & Kenny, Maureen. (2008). Emotional Abuse in the Classroom: Implications and Interventions for Counselors. Journal of Counseling & Development. 86. 10.1002/j.1556-6678.2008.tb00619.x.

It all starts with the infamous "Red-Light Behavior Chart" hung on the board in the front of almost every elementary class. Each student is assigned a clip that is a physical representation of their "good" or "bad" behavior for all the world to see. Green meant that you were "good," yellow meant that you were "okay," and red meant that you were "bad." While many teachers were told to use this or many other forms of "behavior charts," at the root, all behavior charts are simply a way to publicly shame children for not conforming to another's expectations.

In my high school classroom, I was told that if a student misbehaved, then I should write their name on the board as a warning. If they misbehaved again, they would get a check. If they got three checks, then they got in trouble of some kind (usually a threat to involve some type of authority figure or a loss of freedom). I regret to admit that I continued this practice for a few years even though I knew intuitively that I was demeaning and humiliating my students.

My mentor teacher was the one who told me to use that strategy, so I felt as though she had to know best – after all, I was the "young and naïve" teacher, and she was the "expert" who had spent more years teaching than I had been alive. My optimistic heart believed that problems could be resolved through respectful communication and mutual understanding instead of public shaming, but that is not so in the world of school.

Respectful communication requires a large amount of time and emotional investment which the scope and sequence pacing guide does not allow for. So, in the name of "efficiency" and "time management," we resort to practices that we know cause harm because "they work." But what exactly do I mean when I say that these kinds of demeaning and humiliating practices "work?"

Humiliation can be a great motivator. After all, consider the times that you have done or not done something out of a fear of being humiliated. Is it possible to manipulate someone else's behavior, actions, or choices through humiliation or even simply the threat of humiliation? Absolutely. But just because we *can* does not mean that we *should*.

Humiliation only works through extrinsic motivation, but character and integrity are built through intrinsic motivation. Do we really want to create a society where people only do what is right because they are afraid that they will be punished if they don't? Or would we rather create a society where people do what is right simply because it is right, and they earnestly desire to do the right thing? Do we want to create a society where people are motivated by fear of punishment or retaliation, or where people are motivated by love and compassion?

Another way that toxic teachers attempt to "motivate" students through humiliation is through fear of failure and making them feel like failures. I have seen many a "good student" spending hours studying after school for a meaningless quiz not because they love the content or they are passionate about learning, but rather because they are simply afraid to fail. Failure in school is viewed as the ultimate humiliation for a child.

The first school that I ever taught at adopted the motto: "Failure is not an option" – which was a bit ironic because 60% of the students were failing reading and 78% were failing math. Failure is absolutely an option. In fact, it's an essential part of life. But we have attached so much negative stigma to failure that we do not see the value in our failures. Failing does not mean that you are a failure, however many children are not able to distinguish the difference.

I have seen many teachers hang posters in their classrooms of Thomas Edison's famous quote: "I have not failed. I've just found 10,000 ways that won't work." However, I wonder if that same teacher would praise a student sitting in their class for "finding 10,000 ways that won't work." Failure has become something to avoid at all costs rather than a sign that learning is happening. There is always something to be learned through failure, and that is why Thomas Edison was able to state that he had *not* failed.

We must continue to adopt a growth mindset when it comes to children and ourselves because a person who is not afraid of failure is a person who will find success in all areas of life. A person who is free from fear will not be able to be forced or coerced by toxic, abusive people. And we, Toxic Teachers, must stop trying to make our students feel like failures for failing.

But it's not only the children that feel like failures for failing. Parents also feel a large amount of shame and humiliation if they have a child who is failing in school. A parent of a failing child is often labeled as lazy or apathetic. Failing in school does not simply mean getting a failing grade. For many parents, "failing" looks like not have straight A's or getting a C. There is a certain level of shame that parents feel if their children are not performing at the level that *they* deem necessary for them. As parents, we put pressure on our children to not fail – not meet our expectations – because we assume that our child's failure says something about *us* as parents. The pressure and expectations that we place on our children is a direct result of the pressure and expectations that we place on ourselves.

Do not assume that teachers are exempt from this kind of "pressure to pass." A teacher that has a large number of "failing students" is often deemed a failing teacher. Many teachers internalize a student that fails their class as a sign that they are not a good teacher – and with good reason. Many teacher evaluations are based (in part) on student performance. Demeaning and discrediting a teacher based on their students' grades is the equivalent of demeaning and discrediting a doctor based on his patients' BMI. But I will tell you that the best teacher that I ever had – my 11th grade Advanced Placement (AP) English teacher – was the first and only one to give me a D. And the worst teachers that I ever had were the ones that gave out the easy A's.

EMOTIONAL ABUSE

We must stop demeaning others and ourselves for failure. Failure is not good or bad. How we *respond* to failure is what makes all the difference. So "fail forward" with the confidence that our failures will be our steppingstones to success. There is no humiliation in a perceived failure if we can learn to view every failure and every mistake as an opportunity to learn something new.

DISCRIMINATING

Another aspect of emotional abuse is **discriminating** and biased behaviors. I could tell you countless ways that Toxic Teachers discriminate against students due to their age, race, language, culture, religion, or ability level. Oftentimes, the students that are most discriminated against are the ones that need the most love and care and support – in particular, students with special needs and English language learners.

As an ESOL teacher, I saw students labeled as "stupid" or "slow" simply because they could not communicate in English. Toxic Teachers would speak to English language learners with that obnoxious, demeaning tone that many Americans use when communicating with foreigners – that is *if* they talk with foreigners at all. Many Toxic Teachers also choose to overlook the English language learners in their classrooms by refusing to allow them to participate as their peers do because it may "take too long" or they assume that English language learners are not capable of participating in class with everyone else.

As a special education teacher, I have seen students with special needs isolated from their peers in "pull out groups" and "interventions" that make them feel even more "separate" and "different" than everyone else. Students with special needs find themselves in trouble far more often than students without special needs. Instead of learning to treat students with special needs with care and compassion, a Toxic Teacher is quick to punish and isolate.

I would be remiss if I did not also address the fact that many students are being discriminated against by being labeled and tracked as having "special needs" when, in reality, they are simply normal children that refuse to be confined to the box that a Toxic Teacher deems appropriate for them.

The special education program has become the primary vehicle for discriminating against boys (especially African American and Hispanic boys). Even though boys and girls are equally distributed in schools, approximately 67% of the students in special education programs are boys. Only 33% of the students in special education programs are girls.[5] Why is that?

---

[5] Schaeffer, K. (2020, July 27). *As schools shift to online learning amid pandemic, here's what we know about disabled students in the U.S.* Pew Research Center. Retrieved October 25, 2021, from
https://www.pewresearch.org/fact-tank/2020/04/23/as-schools-shift-to-

Why do we have a disproportionate number of boys being labeled as having Attention Deficit Hyperactivity Disorder (ADHD)? Because it is easier to discriminate against a child who won't sit in his seat because he loves to run and label him with ADHD instead. It is easier to discriminate against a child who refuses to do a boring math worksheet because he would rather color on his desk instead. It is easier to discriminate against a child who would rather stare out the window dreaming of his freedom and creating adventures in his head than to stare at a Toxic Teacher talking at him all day long about a topic he cares little about.

Boys are overrepresented in every single special education category (except for deaf and hard of hearing). Boys comprise 67% of the children labeled as having Oppositional Defiant Disorder (ODD). Boys comprise 73.4% of the children with a Specific Learning Disability (SLD). Boys comprise 76.4% of the children with an emotional disability.[6] Whether this is an issue of biology, behavior, or bias is still up for scientific debate, but speaking from experience, many (not all) of the children that we label as having "special needs" are just children that have normal needs – to be loved, respected, and cared for. They are

---

online-learning-amid-pandemic-heres-what-we-know-about-disabled-students-in-the-u-s/.

[6] Wehmeyer, M. L., & Schwartz, M. (2001). Disproportionate Representation of Males in Special Education Services: Biology, Behavior, or Bias? *Education and Treatment of Children, 24*(1), 28–45. http://www.jstor.org/stable/42899643

TALES OF A TOXIC TEACHER

children that have normal needs – to be curious, passionate, and free.

We would rather discriminate and label a child as "disabled" or "disordered" rather than take the time to appreciate their uniqueness and allow them to explore the curiosity, passion, and freedom that makes him (or her) unique. We would rather discriminate against a child for not meeting our expectations than to simply free them from those expectations – which really are just limitations of a Toxic Teacher in a Toxic System. Our children were not meant for those systems anyway. Children are meant to be valued for the unique individuals that they are – not the individuals that we want them to be.

Discrimination in schools does not stop with English language learners or students in special education programs. Now, due to COVID regulations, discrimination is showing up in the school systems in new ways. Toxic Teachers are discriminating against children due to their medical or religious beliefs about forced masking, forced vaccination, and forced testing.

Many people have erroneous labeled me as an "anti-masker" or an "anti-vaxxer," but the truth is that I am neither. I am pro-freedom and pro-science through and through. It is precisely because I am pro-freedom and pro-science that I am daring to question the narrative that has been spewed on all of us but especially upon our children.

EMOTIONAL ABUSE

As a teacher, I am trained to be data driven. Teachers are expected to collect data about the children in our classrooms and then make informed decisions based on that data. So, now it's your turn. Let's do something together that the mainstream media, teachers unions, and corrupt politicians would never ask you to do – let's look at the data.

On the next page, you will find the statistics from the Center for Disease Control (CDC) regarding the total number of COVID-19 cases in the United States as of October 14, 2021. There were 5,199,905 cases of COVID-19 in children aged 0-17.

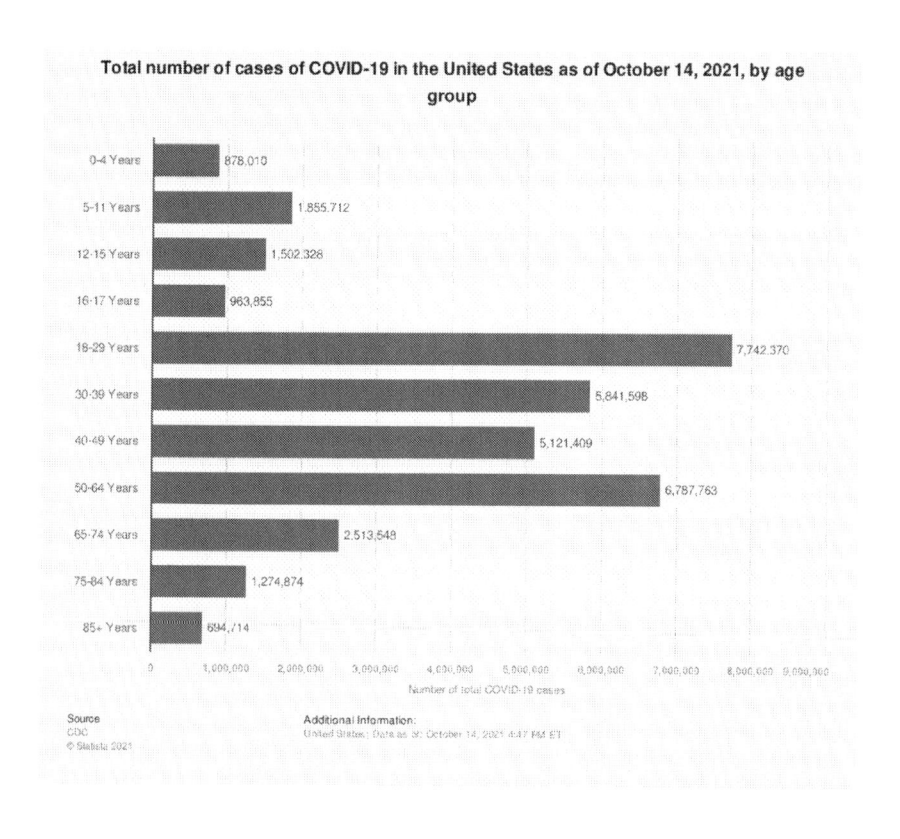

Total number of cases of COVID-19 in the United States as of October 14, 2021, by age group

Age Group	Number of cases
0-4 Years	878,010
5-11 Years	1,855,712
12-15 Years	1,502,328
16-17 Years	963,855
18-29 Years	7,742,370
30-39 Years	5,841,598
40-49 Years	5,121,409
50-64 Years	6,787,763
65-74 Years	2,513,548
75-84 Years	1,274,874
85+ Years	694,714

Source: CDC
© Statista 2021

Additional Information:
United States; Data as of October 14, 2021 4:17 PM ET

TALES OF A TOXIC TEACHER

Over 5 million children have tested positive for COVID-19. But as we all know, the number of COVID-19 cases does not necessarily mean that people are dying or even that they were sick or had any symptoms. So, of the 5,199,905 children that tested positive for COVID-19, how many actually died?

Below is a table showing the number of people who died *with* COVID-19 (not necessarily *from* COVID-19) in the United States from January 1, 2020 to October 13, 2021. Over the course of almost 2 years and over 5 million cases, there have been just 513 deaths for children 0-17.

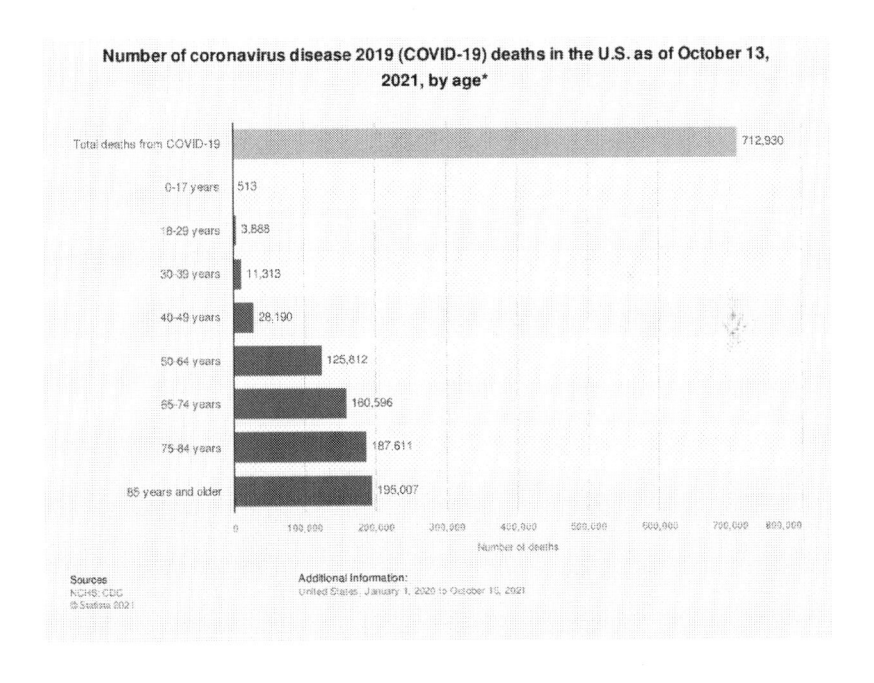

Number of coronavirus disease 2019 (COVID-19) deaths in the U.S. as of October 13, 2021, by age

Age group	Number of deaths
Total deaths from COVID-19	712,930
0-17 years	513
18-29 years	3,888
30-39 years	11,313
40-49 years	28,190
50-64 years	125,812
65-74 years	160,596
75-84 years	187,611
85 years and older	195,007

Sources: NCHS; CDC; © Statista 2021
Additional Information: United States, January 1, 2020 to October 13, 2021

To put that number in perspective, there were 486 children aged 0-17 that died from influenza during the "2019-

EMOTIONAL ABUSE

2020 flu season" which spanned just six months from October 1, 2019 through April 4, 2020. Children are more at risk of dying from the flu than they are of dying from COVID-19, and yet we have never taken any of these extreme measures in the past even though the risk to children was much higher.

Many people have argued that we must force and coerce children to wear masks, get vaccinated, and undergo invasive testing not to protect them because the data is clear that children are of no statistically significant risk whatsoever. Instead, we are told that we must force and coerce children to do all these things in order to protect the elderly people that may live with them. However, according to the CDC, if you are less than 65 years old, you have a 99% natural recovery rate.

On the following page, you will find a chart that I made that would show the statistics about COVID-19 risks and recovery per the CDC to help put this into perspective.

TALES OF A TOXIC TEACHER

Age	Population	Cases	% of Pop.	Deaths	% of Cases	% of Total Pop.
0-17	72,822,113	5,199,905	7.1%	513	0.01%	0.0007%
18-29	42,687,848	7,742,370	18.1%	3,888	0.05%	0.009%
30-39	40,141,741	5,841,598	14.6%	11,313	0.2%	0.03%
40-49	43,599,555	5,121,409	11.7%	28,190	0.5%	0.06%
50-64	58,780,854	6,787,763	11.5%	125,812	1.9%	0.2%
65-74	21,713,429	2,513,548	11.6%	160,596	6.4%	0.7%
75-84	13,061,122	1,274,874	9.8%	187,611	14.7%	1.4%
85+	5,493,433	694,714	12.6%	195,007	28.1%	3.5%

Look at these statistics. Really *look* at them. Consider all the emotional and psychological trauma that we have caused an entire generation because of these numbers. And honestly, ask yourself: was it worth it?

This book is not about COVID-19, and I do not want you to dismiss the overall message of this book because I am choosing to share these numbers with you. But I want you to know that these numbers are the reason that I – and so many others – are being fired from jobs and careers that we love and have given our lives for. These numbers are the reason why student athletes around the country are being discriminated against and denied the right to play their sports – many of whom are depending on those high school sports in order to qualify for college scholarships. These numbers are the reason why the

Kindergartner will never see her teacher smile. Again, I ask: was it worth it? I believe that it will be.

If these numbers can contribute to the great awakening that is happening around the world, then perhaps it will have been worth it. If these numbers can contribute to thousands of parents taking a critical look at the public school system and seeing the corruption of power and control that has infiltrated our classrooms and perpetuated these cycles of abuse against our children, then perhaps it will have been worth it. If these numbers can contribute to thousands of Toxic Teachers waking up to the abuses that are happening right before our very eyes on a daily basis and work hard to create a new educational paradigm free from those abuses, then perhaps it will have been worth it. Only you can decide.

DOMINATING

The next tactic of emotional abuse is **dominating** and controlling behaviors. When domination is present in a relationship, genuine love and compassion cannot exist. We cannot have a positive, connected, loving relationship with a child while seeking to dominate and control that same child. Domination in the classroom is a sick form of bullying that is expected and accepted. We explored some dominating and controlling behaviors in Chapter 1, but we will see other types of dominating and controlling behaviors throughout the rest of the book.

DESTABILIZING

Destabilizing behaviors are behaviors that undermine stability. There is nothing more destabilizing than the school bell. As John Taylor Gatto wrote, "This is a great mystery to me because thousands of humane, caring people work in schools as teachers and aides and administrators, but the abstract logic of the institution overwhelms their individual contributions. Although teachers do care and do work very hard, the institution is psychopathic – it has no conscience. It rings a bell and the young man in the middle of writing a poem must close his notebook and move to a different cell where he must memorize that man and monkeys derive from a common ancestor." It is psychopathic and abusive to deprave a hungry mind of questions and answers with the sound of a bell.

How can a child find stability when we shuffle them from activity to activity every 30-45 minutes? How can we expect a child to explore the depths of any subject that captivates their interest if we communicate through the sound of a bell that no subject is worth investing significant time and energy into? How can we convey the beauty of concentration and perseverance in curiosity if we train our children to stop whatever meaningful work they might be doing at the sound of a bell?

The school bell not only interrupts learning, it also actively inhibits learning for those who do not care much for the tasks they are being forced to do at the time. Much like Pavlov's dogs, we train children to salivate at the sound of the bell because it means a brief moment of freedom from the mundane and meaningless tasks assigned by a Toxic Teacher. How many times do children pack up their work 5 minutes before the bell rings? The school bell has becoming something to look forward to because it means that the pain and boredom of the classroom is almost coming to an end.

Destabilizing behaviors are also intimidating behaviors. We explored various types of intimidation in the classroom in Chapter 3.

DISTANCING

Distancing or Emotionally Unsupportive behaviors are probably the most damaging aspects of emotional abuse from a Toxic Teacher. Distancing may look like sending a child to a "naughty corner," isolating them from the group, or making a child stand or sit away from their peers. Toxic Teachers withhold love and compassion by refusing to see our students as human beings who are equally worthy of love and compassion and use physical and emotional distance as a way to inflict harm.

A Toxic Teacher will not have compassion for a bad day. They will not seek to understand the root cause of a child's

TALES OF A TOXIC TEACHER

"misbehavior." They will not see that the misbehaving child is not *giving* them a hard time but *having* a hard time. They will not work hard to listen to the things their students say – and don't say. A Toxic Teacher will be offended by the student sleeping in their class instead of curious about why the child is so tired. A Toxic Teacher will roll their eyes when they see they got "that kid" on their class roster. A Toxic Teacher will ignore a child's cries for help because they have not yet learned to understand that all behavior *is* communication.

One of the worst parts of emotional abuse for me was being and feeling ignored. And yet I wonder how many times I have left my students feeling ignored?

Occasionally, I would ask a question to my students, and a dozen hands would shoot up in the air. And then there was six-year-old Brendan. He would shoot his whole *body* in the air! He would get out of his seat, jump up and down exclaiming, "Me! Me! Me! Pick me! Pick me! I know!"

But I was a "good teacher." I had been trained to ignore the loud and eager child who was excited to share their knowledge with the class and with me. After all, teachers are only supposed to choose the child who is sitting quietly in their seats – just one of the many ways that we silence our students and kill their love of learning and contribution.

Eventually, I watched as Brendan, who was once loud and eager, didn't even bother to raise his hand anymore. After months of ignoring him, he did not even try to participate. He stopped trying. He stopped learning about whatever I was teaching because I had taught him so well that his voice did not matter. His contribution was not wanted if it was not in the way that I demanded. He had learned so well the pain of being ignored.

If you want to see the impact of stonewalling and ignoring children, all you need to do is step foot inside of a high school. It is rare to find a place in which teenagers share the same enthusiasm and excitement for learning that their six-year-old selves once had. A student who believes that their thoughts and opinions are heard and valued will naturally actively participate, but a student who has suffered years of emotional abuse by being ignored and humiliated will withdraw.

The most difficult part about emotional abuse is that it is not obvious. Oftentimes, it is not even intentional. But that does not diminish the harm that it causes. In fact, emotional abuse produces the most destructive consequences of all forms of child abuse.[7][8] A child may recover from physical pain, but he may never recover from the terror, degradation, or humiliation of emotional abuse.

---

[7] Aluede, O., Ojugo, A. I., & Okoza, J. (2012). Emotional Abuse of Secondary School Students by Teachers in Edo State, Nigeria. Research in Education, 88(1), 29–39. https://doi.org/10.7227/RIE.88.1.3

[8] Bolshakov, V, Carlezon, W, Kandel, E., Teicher, M. (2000), 'McLean researchers document: Brain damage linked to child abuse and neglect'. Available at: www.mclean.harvard.edu/news/press/archived/20001214_child_abuse.php (last accessed 14 October 2021).

Now, I do not know of any teacher who intends to emotionally abuse the children in their care, but the reality is that we do. We shame, humiliate, and ignore. We chastise a child publicly for not finishing his work. We write their names on the board when they don't do what we want. We make them fill out behavior charts. We post their work on the wall. We call their parents in front of the class. We look past them as though they don't exist when they are trying to get our attention.

And, again now, due to COVID, children are not only experiencing emotional distance, but physical and social distance as well. Distancing behaviors are a tactic of emotional abusers that permanently alter a person's brain.[9] The damage that physical, social, and emotional distancing will cause on our children will be irreparable.

DIVERSE

Diverse or Negative Attitudes that have a negative impact on class climate are another sign of emotional abuse in the classroom. Many Toxic Teachers are not aware of attitudes that we have that have a negative impact on our students. A Toxic

---

[9] Lobel, J., & Akil, H. (2018). *Law & neuroscience: The case of solitary confinement.* American Academy of Arts & Sciences. Retrieved October 25, 2021, from https://www.amacad.org/publication/law-neuroscience-case-solitary-confinement.

Teacher can be angry, aggressive, apathetic, critical, cynical, depressed, indifferent, intolerant, irresponsible, pessimistic, prejudice, sad, sarcastic, and selfish.

Perhaps we try hard not to show any of these attitudes publicly but spend a few days hanging out in a teacher's lounge and observe the way that many Toxic Teachers talk about children. We label them as "troublemakers" or "bad kids" or "special." We roll our eyes or poke fun. We gawk at their inability to read or write or do basic math. We forget that a "human is a human no matter how small," and the way that we treat the humans in our lives will have an impact for generations to come.

Another problem is that, most of the time, emotional abuse from the lips of a Toxic Teacher occurs behind the closed doors of their classroom – where only children are the witnesses and the victims. Oftentimes children are not taken seriously when they express their concerns of mistreatment by their teachers precisely because parents and other teachers want so desperately to believe that all teachers are good, loving, caring human beings.

When my daughter returned from school complaining that her preschool teacher was yelling at her and her class, I dismissed my daughter's concerns by making excuses for her teacher and trying to give her the benefit of a doubt, "Ms. R was probably just trying to quiet the class to give you all instructions."

I gaslit my daughter, "I'm sure your teacher wasn't *really* yelling. She was probably just speaking firmly." I even blamed my daughter, "What were you doing that made your teacher yell at you?" No one wants to believe that your child's teacher is guilty of emotionally abusing your child. But by gaslighting my daughter and blaming her for her teacher's negative attitudes, I was only adding to the emotional abuse that my daughter was experiencing.

Another issue that makes emotionally abuse so difficult to diagnose is that we do not view emotional abuse as destructive because it has become a normal and accepted way to treat children – both in school and at home. We are also not trained to identify emotionally abusive behaviors, so that makes it difficult to identify emotionally abusive behaviors in others and in ourselves.

We must work hard to identify emotional abusive behaviors in others and in ourselves and to stand strong against emotional abuse in all shapes and forms. If we are not willing to address our own emotionally abusive behaviors against our own children, then how can we expect to stand against the emotionally abusive behaviors and bullying of a Toxic Teacher against our child? We must lead by example.

FAILURE IS SUCCESS IF WE LEARN FROM IT.

— MALCOLM FORBES

CHAPTER 5
Isolation

My daughter attended public Pre-Kindergarten for a few months when she was four years old. To my great disappointment, she came home almost every single day crying. She complained of her teacher yelling at the kids, bullies that would call her names, and being humiliated in front of everyone for not knowing the "right" answer. However, the most traumatic experience for her was the time that her teacher grabbed her forcefully by the wrist and made her go to time out. When she got off the bus that day with a mark on her wrist and tears in her

TALES OF A TOXIC TEACHER

eyes, I knew that I would never send her back to such a toxic environment again.

As a gentle parenting author, I do not use punishments with my daughter. Instead, I allow her to experience the natural consequences of her actions. I have a deep commitment to treat her with kindness, gentleness, and respect – free from force and threats and coercion that we have already discussed in previous chapters.

Well, that's not entirely true. I *did* send my daughter to time out – once. She was a little over a year old and was enjoying some Cheerios in her highchair. When she was done eating, she took a handful of the leftover Cheerios and threw them on the floor.

"NO!" I shouted. "Sophia! Don't put your food on the floor! Food stays on the table."

She looked up at me and then down at the remaining Cheerios on her tray. She smiled as she grabbed another handful of Cheerios and promptly dropped the entire handful onto the floor again! She stared at me as if to see how I would respond. I could not believe that she would directly defy me like that! I felt embarrassed and frustrated, but I tried my best to stay calm.

"When we make a mess, we clean it up." I stated matter-of-factly as I unbuckled her from her highchair and put her down on the floor next to the mess of Cheerios. "Clean up your mess, Sophia."

"No."

ISOLATION

What did she just say to me?! How dare she defy me like that! Who does she think she is to just say, "No!" Oh, she is NOT going to get away with this! I'll teach her not to say "no" to me again!

I grit my teeth together, took a deep breath and again said in a slow, stern voice. "Sophia, clean up your mess now."

"No."

And there it began – our first "battle of the wills." For the first time in my life, I realized that I could not *make* my child do anything. Apart from grabbing her hand, pulling her tiny fingers open, forcing her to grab the tiny Cheerios and dragging her to drop them in trash can, I could not *make* her do what I wanted.

Hitting her did not make sense to me. I remember thinking, "If the only way that I can get my child to do what I want is by hitting her, then what is that communicating about the kind of relationship that I have with her?" I did not want my child to obey me simply out of fear that I was going to hit her, but I was not about to let her get away with such disrespect and defiance.

Now, it was time to add in a threat. I said, "Clean up your mess now or you're going to go to time out."

"No."

I was completely shocked at her behavior as she had never said "no" to me like this before. I grabbed one of her tiny chairs and turned it to face the corner. "Stay here!" I yelled. I put the timer on my phone for one minute because I had heard someone somewhere say that we should put children in a corner for time out for one minute for each year of their age. I turned my back to my daughter, and I heard her start to cry.

One minute passed, and I could barely hear the timer over her sobs. "Okay, Sophia. Clean up your mess."

"No." She exclaimed with tears streaming down her face.

I was not sure what to do in this moment, so I called my older sister for back-up. My sister, Faith, had four children with loads of experience with this. Surely, she would be able to help me do this right.

"Faith, I asked Sophia to clean up the Cheerios that she threw on the floor and she said, 'No!' so I took her to time out and she said, 'No!' again, and I don't know what to do!"

"Take her back to time out for one more minute. Keep taking her back to the corner until you break her will, and she cleans them up."

"Okay… I'll try." I told her with hesitation in my voice.

So, back to the corner Sophia went… over and over, I asked her if she was ready to clean up, and her answer remained the same, "NO!"

After a half an hour, we were both in tears. I could feel the struggle for power and control between the two of us. Neither was winning. Both of us were losing. I realized that I needed a time out, too.

I locked myself in the bathroom and began to think about the situation. I knew that I want my daughter to obey me because

ISOLATION

she loves me and because she knows that I deeply love her. I wanted our relationship to be characterized by love and not by force, manipulation, or control. I wanted to have a connected relationship with my daughter, but instead of connecting with her, I chose to send her away and isolate her. But I wasn't just physically isolating her in time out, I was emotionally isolating her, too.

I came out of the bathroom and knelt on the floor next to her time out chair. "I'm sorry that I left you alone. I love you, and when we make a mess, we have to clean it up. Do you need help?"

Sophia nodded slowly, and I took her hand in mine as we walked back to the mess of Cheerios on the floor. "Can you help me clean up?" I asked her. She reached down without any fighting and grabbed a handful of Cheerios. She looked at her fistful of food and then up at me with a look of confusion.

"Do you know where that goes?" I asked her.

"No, mama."

I realized in that moment that I had given her a command to do something that she had no idea how to do. I grabbed a handful of Cheerios myself and walked over to the trash compactor. As it opened, I threw my handful inside, and then she threw her handful of Cheerios in.

"Great job! You threw your Cheerios in the *basura!*"[10]

---

[10] *Basura* means "trash" in Spanish.

She clapped her hands and jumped up and down with excitement. I knelt down next to her and asked with a smile, "Do you think we can clean up the Cheerios... cheetah speed?"

"Yeah!"

"Ready... set... GO!" We both ran back and forth between the table and the trash compactor as fast as we could. I ran so fast that I slipped on the kitchen floor as Sophia threw the last of the Cheerios in the trash. She ran over and jumped in my lap. We hugged each other and laughed.

When I chose to isolate my daughter, she responded to that isolation with more defiance. But when I chose to connect with my daughter with compassion and kindness, she responded to that connection with compassion and kindness. I saw first-hand that cooperation flows easily from connection. But isolation disrupts human connection.

There is a reason why isolation is listed as one of the tactics used by abusers in the Power and Control Wheel. There have been hundreds of scientific studies done which demonstrate the physical, emotional, and psychological harm caused by isolation[11], and yet for some reason teachers are still imposing this abusive tactic on students.

---

[11] Loades, M. E., Chatburn, E., Higson-Sweeney, N., Reynolds, S., Shafran, R., Brigden, A., Linney, C., McManus, M. N., Borwick, C., & Crawley, E. (2020). Rapid Systematic Review: The Impact of Social Isolation and Loneliness on the Mental Health of Children and Adolescents in the Context of COVID-19. *Journal of the American Academy of Child and Adolescent Psychiatry*, *59*(11), 1218–1239.e3. https://doi.org/10.1016/j.jaac.2020.05.009

Some teachers may call it the "naughty corner." Others may call it the "Quiet Corner," but the impact is still the same. We are isolating children from the group in a way that creates shame and humiliation and disrupts essential human connection.

Children who do not do what they are told are also isolated in detention. I find that lunch or recess detentions are the most common. In detention, a child is deprived of the only real opportunity that they have during the day to have (mostly) free interactions with their peers. They are separated from the group as a way to inflict emotional harm and pain.

Occasionally, children are even forced to isolate in after-school detention. Could you imagine a boss punishing you in a similar way? By taking away the most valuable asset that you have – your time.

On extreme occasions, students are forced to isolate through suspensions or expulsions. Suspensions and expulsions are one more way that we isolate students from the group and deprive them of their right to a free and public education.

To be honest, I never understood why schools suspend children. When I taught in a high school, we would often have students skip class. If they skipped five classes, then they were supposed to lose credit for the class regardless of their grade. And then if they continued to skip, we would suspend them – a form of forced skipping. So, the punishment for missing instruction is… missing more instruction? Who comes up with these bizarre, nonsensical rules?

Why would we not approach a child with curiosity and compassion instead? Why would we not try to understand the root cause of the behavior? Perhaps they need to skip school in order to work to help their family pay the bills. Or perhaps they simply aren't interested in whatever the teacher is teaching. Or perhaps they understand intuitively that the only way to be free from a toxic environment is to escape.

Toxic Teachers not only isolate the "bad kids," we isolate *all* kids by controlling what they do, where they go, who they talk to, what they read, and more. All children in a classroom are isolated from the rest of the world. We trap them for the majority of their day like prisoners inside those four walls. We plan every minute of their day from start to finish with warmups and worksheets, tasks and tests, activities and assessments. We allow them no control over the events of the day.

We control where they go. First to this center and then the next. Or first to English and then to math. Now it's lunchtime, you must stay in a line. Stay in your seats. Sit on the floor now. Recess time!

We control who they can talk to by incorporating "data-based grouping strategies" and seating charts. We isolate children with other people their age. They never experience the benefit of being taught by an older child, playing with a younger child, or singing with an elderly friend. We pretend that we are "preparing them for real life," but where else in the world are people locked up with other people simply based on when they were born?

ISOLATION

We control what they read. I have taught in schools where the textbooks were older than I was. I have also taught in schools where we had access to the internet, but the schools made sure to block certain "questionable" content (typically conservative, Christian, or "conspiracies"). The censoring of information is a dangerous and abusive precedent. We cannot be expected to raise critical thinkers unless we give them access to information that may cause them to think critically about a topic. But schools do not want critical thinkers. A critical thinker may start to ask questions that the system does not want to answer. A critical thinker may cause trouble for the status quo, but if we can just keep children isolated, we can control what they think which will control who they will become.

Schools have also started to impose a new toxic system of isolation. Under the guise of "COVID-19 Safety Guidelines," we are isolating children on a massive scale unlike we have ever seen before in history. A recent study concluded that "social isolation and loneliness [due to COVID-19] increased the risk of depression and anxiety."[12]

Through forced masking, quarantining, and social distancing practices, we are causing children to experience

---

[12] Loades, M. E., Chatburn, E., Higson-Sweeney, N., Reynolds, S., Shafran, R., Brigden, A., Linney, C., McManus, M. N., Borwick, C., & Crawley, E. (2020). Rapid Systematic Review: The Impact of Social Isolation and Loneliness on the Mental Health of Children and Adolescents in the Context of COVID-19. *Journal of the American Academy of Child and Adolescent Psychiatry*, 59(11), 1218–1239.e3. https://doi.org/10.1016/j.jaac.2020.05.009

isolation in a way that will cause great harm to their socioemotional development. From a developmental psychology perspective, we must understand that social skills and emotional skills are indeed distinct, but that both sets of skills coexist and support the development of each other.[13] Developing social and emotional skills is of the utmost importance because that is the foundation for children to be able to recognize emotions in themselves and in others[14] as well as to develop a sense of empathy.[15]

Due to isolation, children may exhibit some or all of the following symptoms:

- Sadness or insecurity[16]
- Anger[17]
- Frustration or Boredom[18]

---

[13] Schonert-Reichl, K. A., Oberle, E., Lawlor, M. S., Abbott, D., Thomson, K., Oberlander, T. F., & Diamond, A. (2015). Enhancing cognitive and social–emotional development through a simple-to-administer mindfulness-based school program for elementary school children: A randomized controlled trial. Developmental psychology, 51(1), 52.

[14] Dowling, M. (2014). Young children's personal, social and emotional development. Sage.

[15] Masterson, M. L., & Kersey, K. C. (2013). Connecting children to kindness: Encouraging a culture of empathy. Childhood Education, 89(4), 211-216

[16] Hawkley, L. C., & Capitanio, J. P. (2015). Perceived social isolation, evolutionary fitness and health outcomes: a lifespan approach. Philosophical Transactions of the Royal Society B: Biological Sciences, 370(1669), 20140114.

[17] Biordi, D. L., & Nicholson, N. R. (2013). Social isolation. Chronic illness: Impact and intervention, 85-115.

[18] Brooks, S. K., Webster, R. K., Smith, L. E., Woodland, L., Wessely, S., Greenberg, N., & Rubin, G. J. (2020). The psychological impact of quarantine and how to reduce it: rapid review of the evidence. The Lancet.

- Disruptive Behaviors[19]
- Sleep Disturbances[20]
- High levels of stress and cortisol[21]
- Anxiety[22]
- Constant worrying and cognitive rumination[23]
- Depression[24]
- Post-Traumatic Stress Disorder (PTSD)[25]
- Low mood or lack of motivation[26]
- Nightmares or wetting the bed[27]

---

[19] Bosch, O. J., & Young, L. J. (2017). Oxytocin and social relationships: from attachment to bond disruption. In Behavioral Pharmacology of Neuropeptides: Oxytocin (pp. 97-117). Springer, Cham.

[20] Simon, E. B., & Walker, M. P. (2018). Sleep loss causes social withdrawal and loneliness. Nature communications, 9(1), 1-9.

[21] Steptoe, A., & Kivimäki, M. (2012). Stress and cardiovascular disease. Nature Reviews Cardiology, 9(6), 360.

[22] Teo, A. R., Lerrigo, R., & Rogers, M. A. (2013). The role of social isolation in social anxiety disorder: A systematic review and meta-analysis. Journal of Anxiety Disorders, 27(4), 353-364.

[23] Ren, S. Y., Gao, R. D., & Chen, Y. L. (2020). Fear can be more harmful than the severe acute respiratory syndrome coronavirus 2 in controlling the corona virus disease 2019 epidemic. World Journal of Clinical Cases, 8(4), 652.

[24] Sanders, R. (2020). ESS Outline: Covid-19, social isolation and loneliness. Special Report Iriss.

[25] Loades, M. E., Chatburn, E., Higson-Sweeney, N., Reynolds, S., Shafran, R., Brigden, A., ... & Crawley, E. (2020). Rapid systematic review: the impact of social isolation and loneliness on the mental health of children and adolescents in the context of COVID-19. *Journal of the American Academy of Child & Adolescent Psychiatry*, 59(11), 1218-1239.

[26] Ibid.

[27] British Psychological Society (BPs) (2020). Advice for Keyworkers Parents: Helping your child to changes due to the Covid-19 pandemic. Retrieved from https://www.bps.org.uk/sites/www.bps.org.uk/files/Policy/Policy%20-

- Clinginess or "being naughtier"[28]
- Changes in their eating patterns[29]
- Little to no interest in talking or communicating[30]
- Low self-esteem[31]
- Diminished self-efficacy[32]

Research also shows that isolation not only damages a child's social, emotional, and mental health, but it also harms their physical health. Isolation is "closely related to morbidity, hypertension, and immune system dysfunction. A sense of loneliness has also been associated with health risks that are equivalent to or exceed that of obesity or smoking 15 cigarettes daily."[33] Isolation – and even simply *perceived* isolation – is

---

%20Files/Advice%20for%20keyworker%20parents%20-%20helping%20your%20child%20adapt.pdf
[28] Ibid.
[29] Stankovska, G., Memedi, I., & Dimitrovsky, D. (2020). Coronavirus COVID-19 Disease, Mental Health and Psychological Support. Society Register, 4(2), 33-48.
[30] Rubin, K. H., Asendorpf, J. B., & Asendorpfz, J. (2014). Social withdrawal, inhibition, and shyness in childhood. Psychology Press.
[31] Urbina-Garcia, A. (2020). Young children's mental health: impact of social isolation during the COVID-19 lockdown and effective strategies.
[32] Ahmad, Z. R., Yasien, S., & Ahmad, R. (2014). Relationship between perceived social self-efficacy and depression in adolescents. Iranian journal of psychiatry and behavioral sciences, 8(3), 65.

[33] Spreng, R.N., Dimas, E., Mwilambwe-Tshilobo, L. *et al.* The default network of the human brain is associated with perceived social isolation. *Nat Commun* **11,** 6393 (2020). https://doi.org/10.1038/s41467-020-20039-w

robustly associated with cardiovascular disease and cognitive decline.[34]

We will never be able to fully grasp the damage that we have caused as a society but especially as educators responsible for the care of children. We must continue to identify practices that cause and create isolation in children. And we must abolish those practices before we destroy an entire generation through our systematic and systemic abuse.

---

[34] White, C. N., VanderDrift, L. E., & Heffernan, K. S. (2015). Social isolation, cognitive decline, and cardiovascular disease risk. *Current Opinion in Psychology*, 5, 18-23.

ISOLATION DISRUPTS HUMAN CONNECTION.

— ANGELA HARDERS

CHAPTER 6
Minimizing, Denying, and Blaming

Perhaps you are reading this book and thinking to yourself, "Now, schools can't really be *that* bad." And you're right. They're much worse. One of the reasons why things are worse than we could imagine is precisely because we spend a large portion of our time and our energy into minimizing the abuse that happens in school, denying the abuse that happens in school, and blaming the students (or the parents or the government or the economy) for the abuse that happens in school.

I get it. I truly do. No one wants to admit that they are the cause of physical and psychological harm to children. No one wants to admit that they themselves are the abuser. No one wants to admit that, even though they have the best of intentions, their mere participation in a toxic system has made them toxic contributors complicit in the most widespread crime against humanity.

Let me be clear – forced schooling is absolutely a crime against humanity. According to the Rome Statute of the International Criminal Court, Article 7, they define crimes against humanity as "any of the following acts when committed as part of a widespread or systematic attack directed against any civilian population, with knowledge of the attack:

(a) Murder;

(b) Extermination;

(c) Enslavement;

(d) Deportation or forcible transfer of population;

(e) Imprisonment or other severe deprivation of physical liberty in violation of fundamental rules of international law;

(f) Torture;

(g) Rape, sexual slavery, enforced prostitution, etc.

(h) Persecution against any identifiable group or collectivity on political, racial, national, ethnic, cultural, religious, gender as defined in paragraph 3, or other grounds that are universally recognized as impermissible under

MINIMIZING, DENYING, AND BLAMING

international law, in connection with any act referred to in this paragraph or any crime within the jurisdiction of the Court;

(i) Enforced disappearance of persons;

(j) The crime of apartheid;

(k) Other inhumane acts of similar character intentionally causing great suffering, or serious injury to the body or to mental or physical health."[35]

Crimes against humanity are *any* of the above-mentioned acts that are committed against *any* civilian population. In the case of forced schooling, the victims are almost every single child within a state's or county's jurisdiction. Crimes against humanity must be *a widespread or systemic attack*. I ask you, what system is more widespread than that of forced schooling?

And while forced schooling may not murder a child physically, it absolutely is responsible for the murder of a child's creativity, curiosity, and compassion for others. One of the most watched TED Talks of all times is a presentation by Sir Ken Robinson entitled: "Do Schools Kill Creativity?"[36] His answer to that question was a resounding, "Yes!" He argued that "creativity now is as important in education as literacy, and we should treat

---

[35] https://www.icc-cpi.int/resource-library/Documents/RS-Eng.pdf
[36] Robinson, K. (2006, February). *Ken Robinson: How school kills creativity* [Video file]. Retrieved from http://www.ted.com/talks/ken_robinson_says_schools_kill_creativity.html

it with the same status." Additionally, Sir Ken Robinson explained, "We are educating people out of their creative capacities... I believe this passionately, that we don't grow into creativity; we grow out of it. Or rather, we get educated out of it."

While forced schooling may not exterminate children physically, it is certainly responsible for the extermination of ideas. As American attorney and author, John C. Wright stated, "I did not call for the extermination of people, but of ideas." This is precisely the call of all government-run schools. Again, if you do not believe me, simply look up the "banned book list" for your district. Ironically enough, one of the most banned books in America is George Orwell's infamous novel, *1984*, in which he wrote about the Thought Police controlling the people saying: "In the end, we shall make thoughtcrime literally impossible, because there will be no words in which to express it." This is exactly what is happening in our school systems today.

The comparisons between the Thought Police and Toxic Teachers working in government-run schools are eerily similar. Orwell also wrote, "Children, on the other hand, were systematically turned against their parents and taught to spy on them and report their deviations. The family had become in effect an extension of the Thought Police. It was." Orwell's concept of the government turning children against their parents and families is again precisely what we see happening in our school systems today.

The next crime against humanity is "enslavement." The International Criminal Court defines "enslavement" as "the exercise of any or all of the powers attaching to the right of ownership over a person and includes the exercise of such power in the course of trafficking in persons, in particular women and children." In essence, a human being is either a slave or they are free. There is no in between. There is no middle ground. Either you are a slave, or you are free.

By definition, compulsory schooling creates slaves because if you are compulsed, you are forced to do something. And if you are forced, then you are not free. And if you are not free, then you are indeed a slave.

Massachusetts was the first state to pass compulsory schooling laws in 1852, mandating public schools throughout the state, certifying schoolteachers, specifying curricula, and enforcing compulsory attendance. Parents who did not comply with forced schooling were threatened with fines or the government taking children away from their parents, in essence, kidnapping them. By 1918, all 50 states had passed school attendance laws, but most states did not enforce them until the 1930s. In the grand scheme of things, forced schooling is a relatively new experiment with less than 100 years under its belt and yet human beings have been creating, exploring, educating, learning for thousands of years without being forced to do so.

We must understand that the way that we do things now is *not* the way that things have always been done. We must also be willing to accept the fact that the way that we do things now may *not* be the best way to get things done. But regardless of your beliefs about the way things are, the way things were, or the way things could be, we must all understand and admit that the method of forced schooling that we have now is indeed a form of Enslavement.

The next example of crimes against humanity is "deportation or forcible transfer of population." It is defined as "forced displacement of the persons concerned by expulsion or other coercive acts from the area in which they are lawfully present." In the case of forced schooling, children are being "deported" or forcibly transferred from their homes into government indoctrination camps known as "schools."

We have already discussed the role that coercion plays within the classroom regarding children, but it is important to acknowledge that parents are also being coerced to have their children forcibly displaced from their homes and placed into schools.

Bryan was one of my students last year during the COVID-19 pandemic. He was kind and quiet, but after one month of virtual classes, he just disappeared. I called his home multiple times to make sure that he was okay, and finally, his father answered. He shared with me that they were immigrants, and he was unable to provide for his family due to the pandemic. Bryan was fifteen years old, and he had managed to get a job making $20 an hour with his older brother at a construction site.

His family had an urgent need for money to buy food more than they needed him to sit in my Biology Zoom class and learn about the food chain.

Even though I absolutely understood their predicament, I found myself saying, "You do know that if he does not attend class, you can be fined $100 per day that he is absent. Not to mention, you can also go to jail."

Bryan was listening to our conversation, and I could hear him say in the background, "Dad, I'll do it. I don't want you to get in trouble. I'll go back to school." He attended for a few days, and then he never returned. He sent me a text saying, "Ms. Harders, please do not get my dad in trouble. I do want to go to school and eventually go to college, but my family needs me right now." Would *you* have turned him in?

The next crime against humanity is "imprisonment or other severe deprivation of physical liberty in violation of fundamental rules of international law." French historian and philosopher, Michael Foucault, said, "Schools serve the same social functions as prisons and mental institutions – to define, classify, control, and regulate people." He is right. The comparison between schools and prisons is difficult – if not, impossible – to deny.

Upon entering both a school and a prison, a free human being is assigned an arbitrary number that will serve as their "identification" for the rest of their stay. They are given a room assignment and a dress code. They must walk in lines and obey orders without question. They are classified by various categories. They are regulated in their activities.

There are limited times when the prisoner is allowed outdoors. In fact, there are limited and specific times for everything – including eating, drinking, walking, talking, sitting, sleeping, even peeing. There is a lack of individual autonomy and freedom. There is an authoritarian structure built on power and control that enforces arbitrary rules that the prisoners have no input in or control over. In fact, the prisoner only serves to be controlled by those in power. Such is the life of both a criminal and a child. Such is the life of both a prisoner and a pupil.

The next crime against humanity is torture. Torture is "when somebody in an official capacity inflicts severe mental or physical pain or suffering on somebody else for a specific purpose."[37] This is precisely what Toxic Teachers do. While few schools in the United States still incorporate physical punishments like paddling for misbehavior, it is important to recognize that torture is not only physical. Torture is psychological. Torture is causing emotional and mental harm.

I must admit that I have never seen children more tortured then when I taught Algebra 2 at our local high school. I don't know what it is about math – or rather the way that we teach

---

[37] *Torture.* Amnesty International. (2021, June 2). Retrieved September 25, 2021, from https://www.amnesty.org/en/what-we-do/torture/.

math – that just feels like torture. Famous psychologist Carl Jung once shared about his own experience with math class saying, "The teacher pretended that Algebra was a perfectly natural affair, to be taken for granted, whereas I didn't even know what numbers were. Mathematics classes became sheer terror and torture to me. I was so intimidated by my incomprehension that I did not dare to ask any questions." Even President Woodrow Wilson once said, "The natural man inevitably rebels against mathematics, a mild form of torture that could only be learned by painful processes of drill."

It was during my first year assigned to teach Algebra 2 that I discovered Paul Lockhart's essay, A Mathematician's Lament.[38] The essay is a vivid comparison of the torture that it would be if we were to teach art or music in the way that we teach math. Lockhart wrote, "Sadly, our present system of mathematics education is precisely this kind of nightmare. In fact, if I had to design a mechanism for the express purpose of destroying a child's natural curiosity and love of patternmaking, I couldn't possibly do as good a job as is currently being done— I simply wouldn't have the imagination to come up with the kind of senseless, soul-crushing ideas that constitute contemporary

---

[38] *A Mathematician's Lament* was so revolutionary for me that I recorded an audio version of the 25-page essay here:
https://www.youtube.com/watch?v=mYGhwTy4B_M&t=580s

TALES OF A TOXIC TEACHER

mathematics education."[39] But math is not the only way that we torture children. Hopefully, you will be able to will begin to identify for yourself the other ways that Toxic Teachers inflict physical and psychological harm upon children as you read the other chapters of this book.

The next crime against humanity is rape. While most teachers are not abusing their authority by raping children, there are Toxic Teachers who have raped or sexually abused the children that are in their care. The Washington Post covered a story in 2016 about a "day care worker who raped toddlers on video."[40] In 2019, a teacher was arrested for "raping more than 20 students."[41] A quick Google search will reveal children of all ages, races, and genders that have been raped by their teachers.

---

[39] Lockhart, P. (2002). A Mathematician's Lament. Retrieved September 25, 2021, from
https://www.maa.org/external_archive/devlin/LockhartsLament.pdf.

[40] Holley, P. (2019, March 30). *Day-care worker who raped toddlers on video actually a 'charming young lady,' lawyer says*. The Washington Post. Retrieved September 25, 2021, from
https://www.washingtonpost.com/news/morning-mix/wp/2016/07/06/day-care-worker-who-raped-toddlers-on-video-actually-a-charming-young-lady-lawyer-says/.

[41] Report, S. O. (2019, June 27). *Teacher held for 'raping over 20 students'*. The Daily Star. Retrieved September 25, 2021, from
https://www.thedailystar.net/country/teacher-arrested-raping-over-20-students-narayanganj-1763275.

MINIMIZING, DENYING, AND BLAMING

While we all want to believe that our children are safe in school, the reality is that there are sexual predators everywhere.

But what exactly is it that makes rape a crime? After all, sex is great. It is the most intimate way of expressing your love for another human being. And yet this beautiful and wonderful act of sex is somehow turned into a vicious and despicable crime. What is the distinction between sex and rape? The difference is *force*. In fact, the difference between *any* interaction between two human beings is not the action itself but the element of force. Force makes the difference between business and burglary, between a trip to the grocery store and a robbery, between a present for a friend and a pickpocket. Force makes the difference (which we have already explored in the third chapter of this book).

The next crime against humanity is "persecution against any identifiable group or collectivity on political, racial, national, ethnic, cultural, religious, gender…" Persecution is hostility or ill-treatment towards someone else because of their beliefs. Government schools around the world are absolutely being used to persecute groups that do not fit in with the government's agenda. In the United States, government schools are being used to push an anti-Jewish, anti-Christian, anti-conservative, anti-male, anti-white, anti-American agenda.

As someone who is both a Christian and a conservative, I can absolutely attest to the fact that it is not safe to be either in most public schools. If you "come out" as a Christian or a conservative, you should be prepared to face persecution. If you are wondering about the things that your children are being taught in public schools across the country, I invite you to take a look at the *What Are They Learning* website: https://whataretheylearning.com/. Parents and teachers are also able to submit examples of the various kinds of indoctrination that are being forced upon our children. It is certainly eye-opening.

When I was in 11th grade, my Advanced Placement (AP) English teacher assigned all of us to write a persuasive essay demonstrating that Islam was a peaceful religion. While the Muslims that I had encountered in the United States were indeed peaceful and friendly, I also was friends with several missionaries in Islamic countries who would write to us in code every month about the horrors committed in the name of Islam – kidnapping, rapes, murders, and more. I had read the Quran, and so I ended up writing my English paper citing several passages of the Quran that indicated that Islam was not a peaceful religion, including:

- Surah 3:151 – "We will cast horror into the hearts of disbelievers."
- Surah 2:191 – "Slay them [disbelievers] wherever you may catch them and expel them from the place which they expelled you. The sin of disbelief in God is greater than committing murder. Do not fight them in the vicinity of the Sacred Mosque in Mecca unless

MINIMIZING, DENYING, AND BLAMING

they start to fight. Then slay them for it is the recompense that the disbelievers deserve."

- Surah 9:5 – "…kill the polytheists wherever you find them, capture them and besiege them, and lie in wait for them at every ambush…"

Needless to say, my teacher (who was a devout Muslim) was a little upset with me. She gave me a 0 for my paper which brought my English grade down to a D. It was the first time in my life that I had ever received a grade less than a B. I was punished not because I was unable to write a persuasive paper, but because I did not write a paper that agreed with her biased opinions.

Now that I am a teacher, I have seen students that are forced to write about and discuss controversial topics like racism and gender. If a student does not agree with the mainstream narrative, they are indeed persecuted by their peers and even their teachers. Teenagers are given bonus points for participating in Black Lives Matter protests and shamed if they do not.[42] White 8-year-olds have been forced to apologize to their peers of color for

---

[42] Veritas, P. (2021, August 31). *Breaking: Pro-antifa high school teacher in California admits communist indoctrination of students … 'I have 180 days to turn them into revolutionaries' … other teachers 'on the same page' … 'there is a reason why these kids are becoming further left'.* Project Veritas. Retrieved September 26, 2021, from https://www.projectveritas.com/news/breaking-pro-antifa-high-school-teacher-in-california-admits-communist/.

TALES OF A TOXIC TEACHER

"being white supremacists."[43] Boys were instructed to wear tape over the mouths in "solidarity" for the ways that males and the patriarchy have silenced women. Even I, as a teacher, was forced to write a paper about how my "white supremacy" has harmed my students. And yet somehow Toxic Teachers cannot see that persecuting a person for being Christian or white or male is just as evil as persecuting a person for being Muslim or black or female.

The next crime against humanity is "enforced disappearance of persons" which is defined as "the arrest, detention, or abduction of persons by, or with the authorization, support or acquiescence of, a State or a political organization, followed by a refusal to acknowledge that deprivation of freedom or to give information on the fate or whereabouts of those persons, with the intention of removing them from the protection of the law for a prolonged period of time." While the State is indeed responsible for the "detention" of children within the schooling system, the parents may know where their children are, but most parents are unaware of what actually happens in their children's classrooms.

I encourage parents to shadow their children for at least one day per quarter. When my daughter first started to

---

[43] *Students forced to "apologize" for being white.* FreedomProject Media. (2020, August 21). Retrieved September 26, 2021, from https://freedomproject.com/blog/2020/08/21/students-forced-to-apologize-for-being-white.

MINIMIZING, DENYING, AND BLAMING

demonstrate anxiety about going to school, I requested to go and observe her for a day. Even though I was a teacher in the same public school system that my daughter was attending, I realized very quickly that public school is *not* public. The principal refused to allow me access to her classroom. I was told that I needed to schedule a meeting with the teacher and notify her in advance. That is simply not true.

"Do you mean to tell me that you are denying me the right to observe my child receiving a PUBLIC education?" I asked.

"Yes, public schools are not open to the public," the principal replied curtly probably not realizing the irony of her statement.

Because I was a teacher, I was well aware of the fact that our county has an open-door policy that clearly states that parents are welcome to observe their children at *any* time, and we are not required to give notice or schedule an appointment. I pulled up a copy of the open-door policy from the district's website on my cell phone and handed it to the principal. "Would you mind telling me please when the open-door policy stated right here on the district website expired?"

She started to stutter a bit. "Um… um… give me one minute."

About 20 minutes later, the principal returned and said that I would be allowed to go back to my daughter's classroom "just this once." It did not take long for me to realize that there was a good reason for her hesitancy. Even with me being present in the classroom, I observed her teacher rolling her eyes at the kids, making sarcastic remarks, and even yelling twice.

Parent, you may know *where* your child is physically at school, but you will never know where your child is emotionally, relationally, socially, mentally, psychologically if you do not take the time to go and see it with your own eyes. It is well worth the effort. After all, *you* are and will always be your child's primary teacher.

The next crime against humanity is "the crime of apartheid" which is defined as "inhumane acts of a character… committed in the context of an institutionalized regime of systematic oppression and domination." While most people consider apartheid to be segregation or discrimination based on race, the true definition of apartheid is simply segregation or discrimination on any grounds – not just race.

In the case of schools, children are systematically segregated from society simply because of their age. In Maryland, as soon as a child turns 5, they are forced to attend school regardless of whether or not they are physically or emotionally ready or willing to do so.

Due to COVID, we are starting to see a new way that schools are segregating people based on a person's medical status. As I write this, my district has announced that all staff members must receive the COVID injection or be fired by the end of the month. All student athletes must also receive the COVID injection, or they will not be allowed to participate in sports. Our county is also forcing only unvaccinated staff and students to quarantine in the event of a potential exposure even though the few people that I know that are currently sick with COVID have all been fully vaccinated.

Please do not misunderstand. This book is *not* about vaccines. It is about abusive and discriminatory policies and practices. Whether you choose to vaccinate or not, we should all be able to stand united to say that staff and students should never be forced or coerced or threatened or segregated if they do not inject themselves with an injection that has not even finished the clinical trials yet. We should all be able to stand united for freedom. As Benjamin Franklin once said, "Those who give up essential liberty to purchase a little temporary safety deserve neither liberty nor safety."

The last crime against humanity is "other inhumane acts of similar character intentionally causing great suffering, or serious injury to the body or to mental or physical health." Many women in abusive relationships choose to remain with their abuser because "at least he's not hitting me." We have been trained to view only physical abuse as "real abuse," but that is simply not true. As I have learned first-hand, abuse can absolutely be mental, verbal, emotional, financial, spiritual, and psychological. And these types of abuse are just as damaging – if not more so – than physical abuse.

As a society, we also seem to have a very poor understanding of the importance of mental and emotional health.

TALES OF A TOXIC TEACHER

American lawyer and motivational speaker Mel Robbins once shared, "Your mental health is everything – prioritize it. Make the time like your life depends on it, because it does." For decades, we have neglected caring for the emotional and mental health of ourselves and our children. But a child's mental health is just as important as their physical health. And your child's mental health is infinitely more important than their grades, their awards, their sports, their college, their career. Your child's mental health is more important than *anything*.

    The damage that forced schooling causes to a child's mental health means that *no one* leaves unharmed – not even the "good students." Even though I have a master's degree, I am just now beginning to see the decades of damage that forced schooling has caused to my own mental health and wellbeing. I can see now that so much of my desire to be a "good student" was due to my own pride in meaningless accomplishments. I equated being a good student with being a good person or a good daughter. I became a perfectionist and a people pleaser. I became disdainful and resentful of those who did not do as well I did. I became frustrated and annoyed with those who were not as "fast" as I was. Instead of looking at my peers as opportunities for collaboration or cooperation, I started to view my peers as threats and my competition. I found myself doing the bare minimum just to get the A. I had become an expert at swallowing facts a few minutes before a test just to be able to regurgitate the answers and forget it all as soon as the bell rang. I tried my hardest to impress my teachers and parents by being a "good student" and always doing what I was told. However, I also spent a good portion of my teenage years struggling with depression after being sexually assaulted... at school.

While it may be painful and difficult to admit, it is of the utmost importance that we as individuals and as a society stop minimizing and denying the abuse that children experience in school. We must stop blaming children for responding in toxic ways to Toxic Teachers in Toxic Systems. We must take responsibility for the crimes against humanity that we have caused and contributed to – intentionally or unintentionally. It is our only hope for change.

Forced Schooling is a Crime Against Humanity!

— Angela Harders

CHAPTER 7
Using Children

Ruby Bridges was only six years old when she made her mark on the world as the first African American student to integrate into an all-white elementary school in New Orleans in November 1960. She was escorted to school by her mother and four federal marshals. She ended up spending her entire first day in the principal's

TALES OF A TOXIC TEACHER

office due to all the chaos from the angry parents outside. The marshals had to escort her to school every single day for the entire year.

To this day, Ruby is still a civil rights activist committed to creating change through education. She said, "Racism is a grown-up disease, and we must stop using our children to spread it." Ruby acknowledged racism is not something that is born in the hearts of children. It is something that they are taught by the adults in their lives. She also acknowledged that adults use children in order to further their own agendas, and this is exactly what happens in school.

In recent years, we have seen a new push to address "systemic racism" in the United States that has ended up fueling the fire for even more racism and division. Most public schools today are teaching and promoting Critical Race Theory (CRT) which emphasizes that "U.S. social institutions (e.g. the criminal justice system, education system, labor market, housing market, and healthcare system) are laced with racism embedded in laws, regulations, rules, and procedures that lead to differential outcomes by race."[44]

Many people have expressed concerns that Critical Race Theory will actually *create* more racism and racial divisions than

---

[44] Ray, R., & Gibbons, A. (2021, August 13). *Why are states banning critical race theory?* Brookings. Retrieved September 27, 2021, from https://www.brookings.edu/blog/fixgov/2021/07/02/why-are-states-banning-critical-race-theory/.

USING CHILDREN

it prevents. And while this may not be the intention of CRT proponents, the reality of its impact is indeed startling.

From public schools claiming that "all white people" perpetuate systemic racism[45] to schools offering "multicultural" graduation celebrations that are segregated based on race, economic class, or sexual orientation,[46] we see more division and hatred in schools now than we saw 15-20 years ago. How are we creating unity by forcing third graders to deconstruct their racial identities and rank themselves according to their "power and privilege"?[47] If we want all children of all races to feel safe and supported, then why would entire school districts launch a campaign against "whiteness in educational spaces"?[48] If Ruby

---

[45] Dailymail.com, H. A. F. (2021, February 24). *Buffalo Schools Claim 'All whites' uphold racism and show kids warnings from Dead Black Children*. Daily Mail Online. Retrieved September 27, 2021, from https://www.dailymail.co.uk/news/article-9293297/Buffalo-schools-claim-whites-uphold-racism-kids-warnings-dead-black-children.html.

[46] *Multicultural graduation celebrations: Graduate registration*. Columbia College and Columbia Engineering. (n.d.). Retrieved September 27, 2021, from https://www.cc-seas.columbia.edu/multicultural/graduateregistration?fbclid=IwAR2mnp8Zdgs0ja7PPBInY0Sbv-0eILOh7O_0GLNOJLuUkG-6R0cCCckVmmg.

[47] Rufo, C. F., Manning, T. R., & Sand, L. (2021, June 21). *Identity politics in Cupertino, California Elementary School*. City Journal. Retrieved September 27, 2021, from https://www.city-journal.org/identity-politics-in-cupertino-california-elementary-school.

[48] *Subversive education*. Christopher F. Rufo. (2021, March 17). Retrieved September 27, 2021, from https://christopherrufo.com/subversive-education/.

TALES OF A TOXIC TEACHER

Bridges knew that racism is a "grown-up disease" 50 years ago, then why are teachers today teaching children that "babies show the first signs of racism at three months old"?[49] The answer to these questions is: *Toxic Teachers in Toxic Schools are using children.*

Using children is one type of abuse from our Power and Control Wheel that Toxic Teachers utilize in order to maintain power and control. I shared in an earlier chapter about the strange yet euphoric feeling that I experienced on my first day teaching when I realized that I had power and control that I had not possessed the day before. While I would never have admitted it out loud, the truth is that I was using children as a way for me to feel powerful and in control.

I used my students to feel good about myself as a teacher. If they performed well, I would feel great! If they did not perform well, I immediately assumed it was because of something *they* did wrong. In fact, when several of my students failed my class, a co-worker praised me for being a "tough teacher."

Toxic Teachers use children in other seemingly harmless ways as well. We use children to "help" us – pass out papers, grade quizzes, clean up the classroom, and more. We use children to "help" us figure out if another student is cheating or lying or

---

[49] *Racism in the cradle.* Christopher F. Rufo. (2021, March 2). Retrieved September 27, 2021, from https://christopherrufo.com/racism-in-the-cradle/.

stealing. We reward children for "snitching" or turning in their peers when they commit some type of offense that results in the guilty party "getting in trouble." After all, that's what a "good citizen" would do.

We even use children against their parents. Teachers are mandated reporters, so we are required by law to report any suspected abuse or mistreatment of a child. We have the power to remove a child from their home with just one phone call. And while I am grateful for the times that teachers have been able to save a child from an abusive home, there are many instances when teachers have gotten it wrong resulting in unnecessary and undue trauma for both the child and their family. I have also heard some Toxic Teachers claim that parents are abusing their children due to their religious or conservative beliefs.

Toxic Teachers use children against their parents in other ways that are meant to create even more division within the family unit. On the following page, I wanted to share a picture of a sign that was posted on the door of the health room in my former school.

MINORS' CONSENT LAW

Do you know your legal rights to seek healthcare *without* parent or guardian permission?

If you are a minor (under 18 years of age) according to Article §20-102, 104 of the Annotated Code of Maryland, **you have the right:**

- to consent for treatment or advice about sexually transmitted infections (STIs) or sexually transmitted diseases (STDs)
- to obtain contraception
- to consent for treatment or advice about your reproductive health
- to consent for treatment or advice about pregnancy
- to consent for treatment or advice about drug or alcohol abuse

If you have any questions or concerns, see the school nurse. Everything discussed will be kept confidential unless life threatening.

USING CHILDREN

Did you know that your child in a public school may:
- Consent to treatment for sexually transmitted infections (STIs) or sexually transmitted diseases (STDs)
- Obtain contraception
- Consent to treatment or advice about their reproductive health
- Consent to treatment or advice about pregnancy
- Consent to treatment or advice about drug or alcohol abuse

...*without your knowledge or consent*?

I, as a teacher, am not permitted to give a student a Tylenol without parental consent, but the school nurse is able to take that same child to get birth control or even an abortion without a parent's consent. How is that possible? Even more importantly, *why* is that possible?

Schools continue to use children in order to further drive a wedge between them and their parents because that is precisely what schools were created to do. As John Taylor Gatto wrote, "No large-scale reform is ever going to work to repair our damaged children and our damaged society until we force open the idea of 'school' to include family as the main engine of education. If we use schooling to break children away from parents – and make no mistake, that has been the central function of schools since John Cotton announced it as the purpose of the Bay Colony schools in 1650 and Horace Mann announced it as the purpose of Massachusetts schools in 1850 – we're going to continue to have the horror show we have right now." We must understand that it was and is the purpose of school to remove children from their parents in order to have them "educated" – or rather, indoctrinated – by the government.

    Horace Mann, the founder and father of public schools in the United States, believed strongly that schools needed to act *in loco parentis* – "in the place of the parents." For this reason, he said, "The new-born infant must have sustenance and shelter and care. If the natural parents are removed or parental ability fails, in a word, if parents either cannot or will not supply the infant's wants, then society at large – the government having assumed to itself the ultimate control of all property – is bound to step in and fill the parent's place." Horace Mann viewed children as the government does – property to be used. And ultimately, he viewed children as property of the State which is a foundational principle in his development of a public schooling system.

    But Horace Mann did not just view children as property, he also said, "Men are cast-iron, but children are wax." He believed that children were easy to mold. It is precisely because children are easy to mold and manipulate and control and indoctrinate that we force them to spend more time in school than anywhere else. The more time that children spend away from their parents, then the greater opportunity that Toxic Teachers within Toxic Schools will have to indoctrinate those children with the ideals that the government deems necessary because a "good student" will one day become a "good citizen" that will do as they are told without asking questions simply because someone who claims to have "power and control" says so.

Instead of viewing parents as partners, Toxic Teachers view parents as problems. Parents are then treated as obstacles to a child's education rather as the original and ultimate source of a child's education. And if you are a parent reading this book, please know that *you* are your child's first and forever teacher. *You* are your child's primary educator. *You alone* have been entrusted with the responsibility to care for and raise your child. Please do so with great caution regarding the other educators that you allow to contribute to your child's education in life.

There is indeed a distinction between education and school. Mark Twain said, "I have never let my schooling interfere with my education." Similarly, Albert Einstein said, "Education is what remains after one has forgotten what one has learned in school." Two of the most brilliant minds in history have readily acknowledged the fact that true education is not found in school. Education *is* life – not preparation for life – because all of life is learning, and we learn best that which we learn with joy.

Going to school, which we erroneously refer to as "getting an education," is nothing more than getting a government-funded *re-education*. Thomas Sowell wrote,

TALES OF A TOXIC TEACHER

"Education is not merely neglected in many of our schools today but is replaced to a great extent by ideological indoctrination." Children in school are re-educated and indoctrinated to learn the lessons that government desires in order to maintain their own power and control. In school, Toxic Teachers are responsible to teach five key lessons:

1. Truth comes from authority alone
2. Intelligence is the ability to remember and repeat
3. Blind obedience and compliance are rewarded
4. Non-compliance is punished
5. Everyone must conform – intellectually and socially

It is because of these five lessons that John D. Rockefeller invested millions of dollars into schools. "I don't want a nation of thinkers. I want a nation of workers." Toxic Teachers may pretend to teach critical thinking skills, but how can we expect critical thinkers tomorrow when we reward children for blind obedience today?

Johann Gottlieb Fitche said that "education [schooling] should aim at destroying free will so that after pupils are thus schooled they will be incapable throughout the rest of their lives of thinking or acting otherwise than as their school masters would have wished." If this is difficult to believe or accept, consider that it is precisely because we are products of this schooling indoctrination system that was meant to enslave our bodies and minds.

True education is incompatible with school. In fact, the most dangerous thing that Toxic Teachers could ever do is to educate people because when people become educated, they can no longer be controlled. Educated people know their own power and exercise self-control as free human beings. Educated people will refuse to surrender their own power and control to others or to use their own power and control over others.

Many people mistakenly believe that schools were created to serve the people, but the truth is that schools were created to serve evil people who desire to use their power and control over our most vulnerable – young children. Lew Rockwell said, "It isn't a coincidence that governments everywhere want to educate children. Government education, in turn, is supposed to be evidence of the state's goodness and its concern for our well-being. The real explanation is less flattering. If the government's propaganda can take root as children grow up, those kids will be no threat to the state apparatus. They'll fasten the chains to their own ankles."

Candace Owens recently wrote a best-selling book called *Blackout: How Black America Can Make Its Second Escape from the Democrat Plantation*. If you haven't figured it out yet, the largest plantation in the country is the public school system, and every student is a slave. James Baldwin wrote, "Education is indoctrination if you're white – subjugation if you're black." But the truth is, indoctrination is subjugation, too.

It is time to emancipate *all* our children and ourselves. After all, there is only one race – the human one.

How can we expect critical thinkers tomorrow when we reward children for blind obedience today?

— AP Hurtarte

CHAPTER 8
Adult Privilege

One aspect of schools that virtually everyone collectively loathes is standardized testing. The children hate it. The teachers hate it. The administrators hate it. I have no idea why we still do it, but we do.

Standardized tests are a source of major anxiety for everyone involved. Children are being told that their entire futures will depend on their performance on this test. Teachers are evaluated and punished based on their students' performance on this test. Parents realize that college acceptance and scholarships depend on their child's performance on this test. Even the school as a whole is graded based on the students' performance on this test.

Standardized tests measure nothing more than whether a child is a good test taker or not. A standardized test can never and will never assess a whether a child will be successful, happy, kind, or compassionate. We foolishly add meaning and significance to a score that is meaningless and insignificant in the grand scheme of things. Even though standardized tests are a completely unnecessary evil, we spend the majority of our time, money, and energy on arranging, administering, and analyzing these tests.

As a special education teacher, I was assigned to administer standardized tests for students who receive extended time. Instead of spending four hours in testing, these poor souls were forced to spend six to eight hours in testing. As I sat the students in their assigned seats, I noticed that it was Jayden's birthday.

"Hey! Happy birthday!" I exclaimed.

"Yeah, this is a *great* way to spend my birthday," he said with a sarcastic smile.

"How old are you today?"

"Eighteen."

"Oh wow! That's an important one! How does it feel to finally be a legal adult?" I asked.

"About the same," he replied.

"Well, I hope the rest of your birthday is more exciting than the next six hours will be." I gave him a high five and a smile, and he sat down to begin his test.

Several hours later, he finished working, raised his hand, and asked, "Ms. Harders, can I go to the bathroom? I'm done with my test."

"Sure." As he stood up to go to the bathroom, I thought, *"How strange... a grown man, a legal adult, just asked me for permission to pee!"*

After all the students had finished testing and left the media center, my co-teacher and I remained behind to clean up. Even though he is a man about twice my age, he too asked me for permission to go to the bathroom. "Can I go to the bathroom for a second?"

It struck me as so bizarre that two grown adult men would ask me for permission to do something as natural and necessary as peeing. I began to wonder if there are other adults in other careers that ask other adults for permission to pee. We have all been taught from a young age that we must ask permission from some authority in order to do practically anything. But who determines who is "authority"?

In schools, we perpetuate this myth that the adults are the "authorities" simply because they are adults. We take advantage of this "adult privilege" as a way to maintain power and control over children. The problem with adult privilege – which is the same problem with any supposed "authority" – is that we take special liberties and give ourselves a license to do things that the "lesser" group is not permitted to do.

We use "adult privilege" when we enforce the rules but do not follow the rules. A Toxic Teacher will take a student's cell phone for texting during class, but then turn around and text discretely on her own cell phone from behind the teacher's desk while all the children are doing their warm-up or perhaps during the after-school staff meeting. A Toxic Teacher will assign a student lunch detention for arriving late to class but will call a co-worker to "cover my class for a few minutes because I hit traffic." A Toxic Teacher will give student a zero for "cheating" because he shared his work with a friend on an assignment right after attending a "collaborative planning meeting" in which a group of teachers share their work with friends. "Rules for thee, but not for me."

We use "adult privilege" when we treat children like servants or like they are "lesser" than we are. We give commands to them without reason or regard, and then we punish them when they don't obey. We deny children basic rights and privileges like the freedom to pee, the freedom to eat, the freedom to speak, the freedom to move, the freedom to breathe.

"HOW DARE YOU QUESTION ME?!" My co-teacher shouted at a female student so loud that it made me jump. "Don't you dare get an attitude with me, or I will call your mama! You don't EVER speak disrespectfully to an adult!"

"I'm not being disrespectful. I just asked you a question," the student replied. I could feel the frustration and tension growing in the room, and I could not help but cringe as I watched the teacher continue to berate this teenage girl. She towered over the student with a finger in her face. She yelled and threatened. She glared and gritted her teeth. To be honest, *I* was scared.

No one should treat another human being with such contempt – especially not for asking a simple question. If an adult had asked her the same question, I guarantee that the teacher would not have responded in such an angry or hate-filled way. However, she felt as though she had a right to speak disrespectfully to a child simply because she was an adult demanding "respect."

Toxic Teachers demand respect without having first earned respect. We should not expect a child to respect us if we have not first proven that we are people worthy of their respect. And we are not worthy of respect simply because we were born first.

In fact, the reason why kidnappings are so problematic is because we have trained children to respect "authority," and we have trained children to view all adults as "authority" – they have adult privilege. We have trained children to listen to and obey adults simply because they are adults. This is a dangerous – and potentially deadly – idea.

Perhaps you have seen some of the social experiments that have been conducted with children at a park or a playground.

TALES OF A TOXIC TEACHER

A man will approach a child playing and say, "Hello! Your mom had to stay at work, so she sent me to pick you up. Are you ready to go?" With a hidden camera in the bushes, you can watch child after child hold hands with this strange man and then proceed to get into his car. Children have this beautiful ability to trust in others and especially, in adults. But not all adults are safe to obey. Many adults use their "adult privilege" to cause severe harm and even death to vulnerable children.

Toxic Teachers are obsessed with the idea that they are the authority simply because they are an adult, and therefore children must be subordinate. The word "subordinate" means "lower in rank or position, a person under the authority or control of another, a person treated or regarded as of lesser importance than something (or someone else)." Make no mistake. The subordination and subjugation of children was the intention of schools from the very beginning.

The founder of the public school system in North Carolina, judge and financier Archibald Douglas Murphey stated in 1816, "...all the children shall be taught in them... in these schools the precepts of morality and religion should be inculcated, and habits of *subordination* and obedience be formed... Their parents know not how to instruct them... The state, in the warmth of her affection and solicitude for their welfare must take charge of those children and place them in school where their minds can be enlightened, and their hearts can be trained to virtue." You must know that if your child is attending a school, it is with the intention of making your child subordinate, under the authority and control of Toxic Teachers in a Toxic System.

Another way that Toxic Teachers use adult privilege in the classroom is by making all the meaningful decisions. Some adult sitting in some conference room somewhere decided exactly what each child needs to learn at every age. They choose the objectives and the assessments. They choose the amount of time devoted to each topic and even the resources that are permitted to be used. They maintain control over all the curriculum decisions because they are the adult.

Then these adults will pass the curriculum down to the Toxic Teacher who is expected to implement this curriculum without deviation and without dissent. Sometimes the curriculum will give a list of "approved books" from which a teacher may choose one or two. Sometimes the curriculum will look more like a script from a movie or play. "Read this page, then ask this question." While some curricula may allow for some "freedom of choice," the truth is that teachers really do not have the kind of freedom that they deserve in the classroom.

We are constrained by the curriculum which means that our students are constrained by the curriculum too. Now, we may pretend to give students the illusion of "choice." We, as teachers, are encouraged to "differentiate" the process or the product. Perhaps students can choose whether to write a paper about Germany or France, Harriet Tubman or Booker T. Washington,

Lions or Elephants, but I wonder how many children would choose to write papers about these topics if they were not being forced or "externally motivated" by the adult in the room.

By controlling the curriculum, the government can control the minds and the hearts of our children. Again, this was the purpose and intention of schools from the very beginning. Socialist and educational reformer Robert Dale Owen wrote, "The system of public education, then, which we consider capable, and only capable, of regenerating this nation, and of establishing practical virtue and republican equality among us, is one of which provides for all children at all times; receiving them at the earliest age... feeding, clothing, and educating them, until the age of majority." He sought to have compulsory uniformity in schools and total government control of the curriculum, but he did not stop there.

"We propose that all the children so adopted should receive the same food; should be dressed in the same simple clothing; should experience the same kind treatment; should be taught (until their professional education commences) in the same branches; in a word, that nothing savoring of inequality, nothing reminding them of the pride of riches or the contempt of poverty, should be suffered to enter these republican safeguards of a young nation of equals."

In 1826, Virginia Federalist and educationalist Charles Fenton Mercer delivered a speech stating "...the equality on which our institutions are founded cannot be too intimately

ADULT PRIVILEGE

interwoven in the habits of thinking among our youth; and it is obvious that it would be greatly promoted by their continuance together, for the longest possible period, in the same schools of juvenile instruction; to sit upon the same forms; engage in the same competitions; partake of the same recreations and amusements, and pursue the same studies, in connection with each other; under the same discipline, and in obedience to the same authority."[50] The subordination of children under the "same authority" has always been the goal of schools.

The first public school that I taught at had a uniform policy. To be honest, it was quite odd to see public school students in the United States forced to wear the same shirt, pants, and shoes. They looked more like prisoners than academics. Supposedly, wearing uniforms was the school's way of avoiding issues with gang violence and gang-identifying colors, but, of course, gang members found their ways to be known outside of their colors or their clothes. In the end, the uniform was nothing more than yet one more way for the children to be controlled and to be subordinate.

Why do we assume that the adult standing in the front of a group of children is the "authority"? Why do we give one adult the right to rule a group of vulnerable, impressionable subjects? Why do we entrust our most precious human beings – our

---

[50] Rickenbacker, William. *The Twelve-Year Sentence: Radical Views of Compulsory Schooling*, San Francisco: Fox & Wilkes, 1974, 5–27.

children – into the care of abusive tyrants? Why do we perpetuate this myth of adult "privilege" and authority? It is precisely because we are products of this abusive and toxic system.

We cannot confess the absurdity of a teacher's authority and subsequent subordination of children because to do so would cause a ripple effect so catastrophic that no government system would be able to stand – and that is the whole point. Every Toxic Teacher who claims to act on behalf of his or her own "authority" or take advantage of their "adult privilege" is demonstrating that he or she has accepted an utterly ridiculous lie: that his or her position as a teacher changes the definition of which behaviors are moral and which behaviors are immoral. And even though this idea is utterly insane, it is rarely recognized as such because even the victims of Toxic Teachers share in this delusion.[51]

It is not moral to force, coerce, threaten, manipulate, intimidate, isolate, enslave, entrap, gaslight, or abuse another human being. However, a Toxic Teacher practices these evil behaviors and more under the guise of some supposed "authority." If another child were to treat a child in such a manner, we would call him a "bully." If another adult were to treat a child in such a manner, we would call him a "criminal." But a Toxic Teacher is given a license (literally, from the state) to treat a child in the same way, and we call him an "educator."

---

[51] Rose, L. (2012). *Most Dangerous Superstition*. Larken Rose.

It is time for us to wake up, open our eyes, look honestly at the abuse that is happening right in front of us, and to stop gaslighting children and ourselves and thus continue the cycle of abuse by Toxic Teachers in Toxic Systems. And while a Toxic Teacher may be the "authority" in her classroom, she too is subject to the orders and whims of those falsely claiming authority over her. She too is subject to her own set of abusers. Every Toxic Teacher is subject to the administrators who are subject to their supervisors who are subject to the school boards who are subject to the state. It is a long chain of slavery, but it is easier to pretend that you are a master than to admit that you are the slave.

> By controlling the curriculum, the government can control the minds and the hearts of our children.
>
> —Angela Harders

CHAPTER 9

Economic Abuse

When I applied to work for the public school system again after swearing that I would never return to the classroom, I was hired as a secretary in the main office of the same high school that I had graduated from. I was barely making minimum wage, but I was grateful for the ability to be able to work hard while at work and then go home and not have to think about any of it until the next day. I worked quickly and efficiently, so I often found myself to be bored out of my mind.

TALES OF A TOXIC TEACHER

Tasks that would take other people the whole day to complete, I was able to finish in an hour. Needless to say, the other secretaries did not appreciate my "work ethic."

My sister helped me to get the job because she also worked in the same school as the School Financial Specialist (SFS) under the supervision of the School Business Administrator (SBA).

A few months after I began, the SBA moved to a different school, and so my sister was promoted to her position. My supervisor called me and informed me that the next day, I would also be promoted to the position of School Financial Specialist. Never mind the fact that it was illegal and immoral for me to work under the supervision of my own sister, but I did as I was told.

I had learned that nepotism is common practice in any government institution – and the schools are not exempt. After all, the administrative secretary was supervising the other main office secretaries – including her wife, her brother's child's mother, and me.

I thoroughly enjoyed working as the financial specialist for the school, even though it was a huge responsibility. I oversaw the money for all the fundraisers, field trips, and bank accounts for the entire school. It was one of the most eye-opening experiences for me to have thousands of dollars flow through my hands each and every day.

I was shocked to learn the "behind-the-scenes" of a school's finances. I began to see schools as the businesses that they truly are, and I learned quickly that children are the greatest commodity in every school system with a high price tag on every head.

At the time when I started teaching in Montgomery County Public Schools in Maryland, I was living in a nearby county – one of the worst in the state. I did not want my daughter to go to school in the county where we lived, so I called Montgomery County's registrar to ask if my daughter would be able to attend preschool in Montgomery County since I was teaching there. With a pep in her voice, she exclaimed, "Sure! She can attend preschool here, but you will have to pay out of pocket since you do not live in the county."

"Oh, okay, that shouldn't be a problem. How much would it cost for her to attend the public preschool program?"

"$15,209."

I almost spit my coffee out of my mouth. "I'm sorry, how much? Did you say 15 *thousand*? Dollars?"

She chuckled. "Yes, ma'am. $15,209."

This prompted me to look deeper into the average cost per student in the United States. According to the 2020 U.S. Census Report, Montgomery County in Maryland (where I now live and work) is the 4th most expensive county in the entire United States paying an average of $16,005 per pupil. New York City pays the most at a whopping $26,588 per pupil.[52] Utah pays the least at $7,478 per pupil.[53]

In Montgomery County, a teacher's starting salary is $51,513,[54] so that means that about 3-4 students will pay a teacher's entire salary for the year. That also means that a classroom of 35 students represents more than half a million dollars of taxpayer money. Every child matters. Every child counts. Every child costs.

Did you know that your child has a bounty on his or her head?

Now, I don't know about you, but if I had to spend $15,209 for my child's education, I would certainly *not* choose a public school. For that amount of money, I could send my child to a private school in which she would be one of just eight children in the classroom (instead of one of thirty). As a homeschooling parent, I could use that money to pay for a private

---

[52] Papst, C. (2020, October 8). *U.S. Census: Six Maryland Schools Among Nation's most funded.* WBFF. Retrieved October 4, 2021, from https://foxbaltimore.com/news/project-baltimore/us-census-six-maryland-schools-among-nations-most-funded.

[53] *U.S. public education spending statistics.* EducationData. (2021, August 2). Retrieved October 4, 2021, from https://educationdata.org/public-education-spending-statistics.

[54] *FY 2021 salary schedules - Montgomery County Public.* Retrieved October 4, 2021, from https://www.montgomeryschoolsmd.org/uploadedFiles/departments/ersc/employees/pay/schedules/salary_schedule_current.pdf.

ECONOMIC ABUSE

tutor or enrichment classes or even to travel and help her learn through incredible life experiences.

Now, parent, I would like to ask you the same question: if you could choose how to spend $16,000 towards your child's education, what would you do with that money?

Withholding access to money that belongs to the student – not the system – is one way that schools economically abuse children and families. We steal your money through taxes and then decide what to do with your money by dumping it into a public school without any input from the public or accountability to the public. Students and families do not have any right to choose how those funds are spent any more than they are free to choose the school that their children will be confined to for the next 13 years.

School choice is a very politicized topic in the United States. People who disagree with giving parents the freedom to choose where and how to educate their children cite arguments like the following:

- Charter Schools are notorious for kicking out hard to teach students
- Charter and Voucher Schools increase segregation
- Charter and Voucher Schools take away funding from traditional public schools[55]

---

[55] Singer, S. (2017, February 19). *Top 10 reasons school choice is no choice.* HuffPost. Retrieved October 4, 2021, from

However, as we see in the private sector, competition *increases* quality. Dr. Corey DeAngelis, an advocate for school choice in the United States, said, "If a private school underperforms, it shuts down. If a charter school underperforms, it shuts down. If a district-run school underperforms, it gets more money." And, he's right. Private and charter schools have an incentive to perform because they know they are directly accountable to families for the results that they produce. In contrast, public schools receive funds without any accountability at all.

I remember at the end of the school year when I was a financial specialist, we had several tens of thousands of dollars that had not been "accounted for." The principal instructed the leadership team to "find something to do with the money because if we don't use it, then we lose it."

I learned that the school's budget for the following year is dependent upon how much money they use from the previous year. If we use $100 million one year, then we get $100 million the following year. But if we use the money wisely, implementing a sound budget, and only spend $70 million for the things we truly need, then the following year, we will only get $70 million. Schools are punished for being economically and fiscally responsible.

---

https://www.huffpost.com/entry/top-10-reasons-school-choice-is-no-choice_b_58a8d52fe4b0b0e1e0e20be3.

ECONOMIC ABUSE

"If we do not use the money, the state will think that we don't need it, so they will give us less next year," my principal explained.

"But if we do not *need* the money, then why would we use it? Can't we put it into a savings account or something?" I asked trying to understand the logic behind this absurd waste of funds.

My principal shook her head. "It just doesn't work like that. We need to find a way to spend it within the next few weeks, or it will be gone."

So, we spent thousands of dollars on pizza for the students, gifts for the teachers, and extra supplies that we did not need, and then we would try to stuff the overwhelming supplies into overflowing closets all around the school building.

As a taxpayer, I found this practice to be utterly shameful.

As a teacher, I found this practice to be utterly abhorrent. I had spent thousands of my own money to buy paper and posters and pens over the years. Many of my colleagues also did the same. I never knew, as a teacher, that schools had money to burn. There was more than enough for the district to buy me paper and posters and pens. But why would the school spend money when there are so many teachers willing to empty their pockets to do so with the money that they have earned through the sweat of their own labor?

There is a reason why schools do not reveal their budgets to the public. If the people knew the way that schools waste taxpayer money, there would be a great upheaval and a demand for accountability and for change. The people who control the money, control the people.

Economic abuse is a reality for many people in abusive marriages. Usually, the husband will use the finances in order to control the wife and hold her hostage in a toxic marriage. He may withhold money from his spouse, only dishing out a meager allowance that is barely enough to survive. He may decide what and how and when the family spends money and refuse to allow the wife to participate in any financial decisions.

Economic abuse is also a reality for students and families in an abusive relationship with the school system. The state controls the finances in order to control the children and families. The state withholds money from children and families by not allowing them to use that money in the way that they deem most necessary or efficient for their own child's education. They make all the decisions regarding the budget with little to no input from students or parents.

Families feel economically trapped into keeping their children in the public school. If they had access to even a small portion of the $16,000 that the state spends per child, I guarantee you that many families would choose to send their children somewhere else (or at least use those funds in a more effective way rather than wasting it on thousands of dollars of pizza).

We believe that public school is free, but we forget that nothing in this life is free. Everything has a cost. While public school may function as free childcare for most families, it is certainly not free.

According to the National Retail Federation (NRF), families are planning to spend $696.70 on back-to-school supplies alone. Several of these supplies are for "community use" like tissue paper, extra pencils, and glue. Parents are expected to help offset costs for classroom supplies since many districts do not provide them. Families are also expected to pay extra for:

- Field trips
- Cafeteria lunches
- Class parties
- Teacher appreciation gifts
- Books
- Class fees
- Parking permits
- Graduation cap and gown
- Dances and prom
- Uniforms
- Sporting equipment
- Club fees
- Fundraisers
- Technology
- Agenda books
- Instrument rental fees
- Transcript fees

- Transportation expenses
- Student obligations for damaged/unreturned items
- Even your own diploma!

While many of these expenses are relatively small amounts, it certainly adds up over 12+ years. And we are not even looking at the cost of colleges and universities!

While schools have many necessary (and unnecessary) additional costs, the most expensive cost of schools is not material. There are hidden costs that we rarely discuss – ones that most people are probably not even aware of.

Schools cost students (and parents) emotionally, physically, personally, relationally, and spiritually. I have shared these costs throughout this book, but it is important for you, beloved reader, to reflect on your own experience and consider the cost. Ask yourself openly and honestly: What has my experience in school cost me?

This was a difficult and even painful question for me to ask myself because I loved school – or at least, that's what I thought. It has only been recently that I have been able to view my own school experience through a new lens and to truly be able to see all the damage that had been done that I was unaware of.

Now, I can see the emotional cost of school in my own life. I remember the constant anxiety that I would feel before and after taking a test. I remember the shame that I felt when a teacher would write my name on the board or when my fellow classmates would make fun of me. I remember the fear that I felt standing before my class giving presentations or when a teacher would call on me to provide an answer that I didn't have. I remember the feeling of frustration when I could not figure out that math problem. I remember struggling with depression and loneliness as a teenager. I remember being bullied by the "cool kids" and having other students gossip and spread lies about me. I remember the stress and pressure that I put on myself to get straight A's, and I remember feeling like a failure if I didn't get straight A's.

As I shared in previous chapters, emotional stress causes physical stress. I struggled with insomnia every night, and then I dreaded waking up early in the morning. I would go throughout my day with low energy and feeling fatigued. I would get headaches or nauseous any time that I was feeling anxious. I started losing my hair. I would experience chest pains and even started grinding my teeth at night due to stress. In fact, psychological stress may exacerbate a "common" teenage problem, acne.[56] Not to mention, I would often get physically ill from being around other kids. I experienced everything from catching a cold to having lice, mononucleosis and the flu. Sitting

---

[56] Yosipovitch, G., Tang, M., Dawn, A. G., Chen, M., Goh, C. L., Chan, Y. H., & Seng, L. F. (2007). Study of psychological stress, sebum production and acne vulgaris in adolescents. *Acta dermato-venereologica, 87*(2), 135-139.

in a chair for 6-8 hours a day contributed to me being overweight. And the fear of being "too fat" has caused many young girls to struggle with eating disorders which can lead to death. Not to mention, the toxic environment of schools is largely responsible for the ultimate physical harm – suicide, which is the second leading cause of death for teenagers today.

School had a personal cost to me. I entered school as an eager, happy, carefree four-year-old girl. I left school as a shell of the girl that I once was. I did not know what I wanted to do with my life because I had spent the last 14 years being told what to do with my life. I wonder what I would have become if I had been given the freedom and the time to explore my own unique talents, gifts, and passions. I was indeed a jack of all trades, but an expert of none. Well, I suppose I wasn't a jack of *all* trades; I wasn't a jack of *any* trade. I left school with a lot of facts and head knowledge, but I was lacking in the real-life skills that I needed to be a successful, independent adult. I had lost my identity as an individual because I excelled at conforming to the expectations of the group. School had cost me personally – because I had lost the person that I was when I began.

School also had a relational cost for me. While I was in school, my parents worked very hard running an insurance business from the basement of our home. And even though my parents were physically at home all day, I did not see them or spend much time with them. They would come upstairs around 5:00 PM, we would have dinner together as a family, clean the kitchen, and then get ready to go to bed by 8:00 PM. While I appreciated the fact that we had dinner together as a family, I know that this practice is no longer common practice in our society today. Most of my students have expressed that they do not have dinner with their family members. In fact, many of them rarely even see their parents because they are working so hard. A lack of quality time with the people in your life will cost you a quality relationship with that person. What a shame that our children will miss out on a relationship with us, as parents, because, for most of their lives, we send them away.

Schools not only cost children a relationship with their parents, but they also cost children their relationship with God. The Barna Research Group discovered that one out of nine young people who grow up with a Christian background will lose their faith in Christianity.[57] After high school, 66% of young adults that regularly attended a Protestant church in high school say that they have stopped attending church between the ages of 18 and 22. It is extremely difficult to be a child and a Christian in school.

Many Christian parents may argue that we are called to be "light in the darkness," and while that is true, that is not the job for your five-year-old or even our fifteen-year-old. We have been

---

[57] *Five myths about young adult church dropouts*. Barna Group. (n.d.). Retrieved October 13, 2021, from https://www.barna.com/research/five-myths-about-young-adult-church-dropouts/.

entrusted by God with the responsibility of teaching our children. No teacher – no matter how many degrees or years of experience – can ever replace you, the parent, as your child's primary teacher. We simply cannot afford to hand over that responsibility to a complete stranger.

You will also find that the economic cost of your education does not begin to compare to the emotional, physical, personal, relational, and spiritual cost – whether you went to public or private school. We know that private schools are not free, but public school is not free either. The cost is greater than you could ever imagine.

Children are the greatest commodity in every school system with a high price tag on every head.

—ANGELA HARDERS

CHAPTER 10
The Antidote

One child, one teacher, one pen, and one book can change the world. My hope and prayer is that this would be true for this book that you hold in your hands right now. I know that this is not an easy book to read. It confronts some of our most deeply held beliefs about life, about government, and even about ourselves.

It was an incredibly painful process for me to realize that I was a Toxic Teacher in a Toxic System. While I had hoped that I might be able to reform the system of schools from the inside-out, the truth is that the only way to be free from an abusive relationship is to leave. *Now* is the time to leave.

As I have said many times before, the problem is not that schools are broken, the problem is that they are working perfectly as they were designed. It is not that schools have failed, but that they have succeeded in their primary mission – to enslave the hearts and minds of entire generations. The chains of being confined in the classroom have made slaves of us all.

We attended school in hopes of drinking from the age-old fountains of wisdom. However, forced schooling has poisoned the well of lifelong learning. We have all been given a lethal dose of coerced learning that has killed our creativity, curiosity, and compassion for those around us.

So, what is the antidote for a Toxic Teacher in a Toxic System?

Freedom.

We must break free from "the way that things have been done." We must begin to question everything and to find our own answers. We must begin to dream of a world that is free from abuse and violence – and we must work diligently towards that end.

Now is the time.

Now we must choose for ourselves and our children: liberty or death. And if for a moment you assume that I am being dramatic or exaggerating that schools are indeed a system of slavery, consider the fact that we trap our most vulnerable children inside a building for over thirteen years, isolate them from their families and friends, restrict their movement, limit their activities, deny them the right to speak freely, force them to complete tasks against their will, punish them when they don't or won't or can't, categorize and label them, manipulate them, bribe them, use them, abuse them, kill their creativity and individuality, and pretend "it's for their own benefit" – or rather for the "greater good."

Recently, I learned that Harriet Tubman was born a slave on a plantation about an hour and a half from my home in Maryland. Since I am passionate about experiential life learning, I decided to take a group of children to the Harriet Tubman Museum in order to learn more about Harriet, her fight for freedom, and the history of slavery in our state.

Upon entering the museum, there was a huge statue of Harriet Tubman with the following words etched behind her: "I reasoned this out in my mind, there was one of two things I had a right to, liberty or death; if I could not have one, I would have the other." Harriet understood that death was better than slavery, and she was willing to risk her life in order to obtain her freedom. Life without freedom is not a life at all.

However, part of our struggle today is that we do not see ourselves – or our children – as slaves. We mistakenly believe ourselves to be free. It is easier to identify a slave by the chain around his neck or his hands or his feet. It is much more difficult to identify a slave by the chain around his mind or his passions or his dreams. Euripides said that to be a slave is "to be abused and bear it," and this is exactly what is happening in our schools. Students and teachers alike are being abused and asked to "bear it." And it's time to say, "No more!"

So, while it is awful to be a slave, it is even more awful to be a slave and to not know you are a slave. Frederick Douglass once said, "I didn't know I was a slave until I found out I couldn't do the things I wanted." Consider for a moment all the things that a child longs to do but cannot because of Toxic Teachers in a Toxic School. A Toxic Teacher is nothing more than a slave master forcing children to become slaves of the ideals and ideologies of an abusive government system.

Before we can stand for our freedom, we must first admit that we have been enslaved. Freedom philosopher and voluntaryist, Larken Rose, wrote, "People who consider themselves educated, open-minded, and progressive do not want to think of themselves as the slaves of a master." No one wants to admit that he is a slave any more than I wanted to admit that I was a Toxic Teacher. And yet we must be brave enough to admit the truth about a problem before we can begin to address that problem.

As I learned more about Harriet Tubman's story, I also was surprised by the fact that as she was escaping with her brothers, both of them changed their minds and decided to turn back. They had an opportunity to be free, but instead they chose to return to their masters and to their life as a slave. Why would a slave ever return to their master?

There were slaves that chose to remain slaves because their masters provided them with food and shelter. Some slaves chose slavery because they were afraid of the risks that came along with freedom. For some, the trauma bonding between slave and slave master had reached a point that Frederick Douglass, a former slave, wrote that many slaves were "proud of how hard they worked for their masters and how faithfully they did as they were told. From their perspective, a runaway slave was a shameful thief, having 'stolen' himself from the master."[58]

Trauma bonding is a unique phenomenon that occurs in abusive relationships where there is a persistent cycle of abuse. There are times when the abuser seems to treat the abused well, so it becomes difficult to leave because we want to believe and hope for the best. There is a strong emotional attachment between the abused and his or her abuser as a result of this cycle of abuse and violence intertwined with some semblance of kindness. This is the reason why a slave will return to his master, an abused wife will return to her abusive husband, or a parent will send a child back to an abusive school. We are trauma bonded slaves.

---

[58] Rose, L. (2011). *The Most Dangerous Superstition.*

TALES OF A TOXIC TEACHER

If you find yourself excusing or justifying the abuse that I have shared in this book, consider that that is evidence of the trauma bonding that you yourself have experienced. You will know that you have been trauma bonded when you are so attached to a toxic person (or system or idea) that you are willing to maintain a relationship, even at the expense of yourself (or in this case, your child) for the few and far between "highs." There is an actual addiction that occurs in the brain due to the constant cycle of rewards and punishments creating oxytocin, dopamine, norepinephrine, and serotonin.

Again, this explains why so many people remain attached to the idea of "school" and struggle to let it go – even though they see the damage that forced schooling has caused in themselves and in their children. We hold on to "fond memories" of school as a way to excuse or dismiss the terrible ones. We do not want to admit the abuse that we have endured or that perhaps something that society perceives as good could in fact be evil. We cannot cause blind eyes to see that if you are forced, you can never be free.

I hope that by now you have become convinced that even those of us with the most positive experience in school have not managed to escape unscathed. We all bear the wounds of our slavery. We all hold the harm of the cycles of abuse.

Freedom begins in the mind. Just as Harriet Tubman imagined a life where she would be free from slavery, we too can begin to imagine a life where we can be free from forced schooling. Imagine for a moment a world without school. If school did not exist, what would you do? How would you spend your time? What would you want to learn about? What skills would you want to cultivate? If you were free from force and coercion, what would you create?

Those questions are the beginning of a journey headed towards educational freedom. Some may call it self-directed learning, life learning, or unschooling. I prefer to call it "Peaceful Worldschooling," but the principle is the same – *freedom*.

I have been pursuing and advocating for educational freedom for myself and my children for years, and it has been the most exhilarating journey of my entire life. I invite you to do to the same. Remove the chains of "should" from your shoulders:

- I *should* learn this
- I *should* learn in this way
- I *should* learn in this time
- I *should* learn in this place
- I *should* learn at this pace
- I *should* learn from this person
- I *should* learn from this workbook
- I *should* learn from this book
- I *should* get this grade
- I *should* take this test
- I *should* do and be xyz

When we remove the chains of "should," the whole world of true freedom will open up for us and our children. We will no longer be bound by the expectations of another, but rather we will begin to set expectations for ourselves and work hard to reach them. After all, this is the goal of true education for life – self-motivated, self-initiated, self-directed learning.

After we have a vision of freedom in our minds, then we can begin to create the life we desire and take action that is consistent with that vision. When you are ready to take action, there are three main steps that I would advise to be free from the Cycles of Abuse in School: (1) Leave School, (2) Deschool, and (3) Worldschool.

1. Leave School

As I said before, the only way to be free from an abusive environment is to *leave.* In the same way that Harriet Tubman needed to flee in order to be free, I implore you to do the same: stop sending your children (or yourself) back into those same cycles of abuse within the school system. Be willing to stand for your child's freedom and your own. Be brave enough to leave behind the systems that were intended to enslave us. Be bold enough to invite others to join you on this new journey to freedom.

While many families leave school to homeschool, I actually do *not* recommend homeschooling. The reason for that is because homeschoolers are still under the control and jurisdiction of the state. The state still tells parents what and how to teach their children. This is why even homeschool families need to report to the state or have their child's learning reviewed by the state every year. So even though your child is not registered in a public school, they are still technically being educated in the "public domain" under the supervision of the state.

Instead, we need to learn to educate our children in the private domain through the use of a Private Education Association (PEA) or a Private Ministerial Association (PMA). I could write an entire book on this topic (perhaps, one day I will), but if you are interested in an immediate solution to having educational freedom for you and your children, please visit my website: www.peacefulworldschoolers.com. By becoming a member of my PMA (or even by creating your own), you will be able to restore complete educational freedom for your family.

Parents are and will always be the primary educators of their children. Educating our children is our God-given right and responsibility. I am honored to help support you in your educational freedom journey.

2. Deschool

After you leave school, then you need to *deschool*. Deschooling is a process by which you unlearn all the things that you have learned about learning. In essence, you live as though school does not exist.

Pretend that every day is Saturday. Cook. Clean. Relax. Watch a movie. Read a book. Play a game. Go on a walk. Visit a museum. Spend time with friends. Go somewhere special with someone special. Do something you love.

I recommend that you spend at least one month deschooling for every year that you have been in formal schooling. For example, if your child is starting 2nd grade, then they will need approximately 2 months of deschooling (one month for Kindergarten and one month for 1st Grade). In my case, I have a master's degree, which means that I have been in formal schooling for over 20 years. Plus, all the years that I was in school as a teacher, and I will need to spend over two full years deschooling myself as I begin this journey towards educational freedom.

During the deschooling process, let go of any expectations or semblance of "school." Set aside the curriculum. Do not worry about the worksheets. Give up on the grades. Throw away the tests. Just be.

Instead, focus on connection instead of correction. Focus on laughter instead of lessons. Focus on pursuing passions instead of pointless projects. Focus on life and love and living and loving together. Focus on peace and purpose. Focus on fun and faith. Focus on you and the person that you want to be in the world with your child.

3. Worldschool

This is where the fun begins. Many people have come before me and written about different ideas for educational freedom for children. Maria Montessori advocated for child-led learning in the Montessori method. Daniel Greenberg wrote about educational freedom as the foundation for democratic Sudbury Schools. Rudolf Steiner shared the power of self-initiated play in nature through the Waldorf Method. John Holt is the father of the modern unschooling movement.

While unschooling resonated the most with me, I was not a fan of the term. I wanted to create an educational approach that clearly communicated the principles that I was standing for – and not just the principles that I stand against (namely, forced schooling). I decided that my family and I would be *Peaceful Worldschoolers*.

Peaceful Worldschoolers are people that are committed to cultivating peace in the world beginning right in our own hearts and homes. We view the world as our biggest and best classroom, and the people and places in it as our greatest teachers. We view all of life as learning and all learning as valuable. If you would like more information about Peaceful Worldschooling, I invite you to read my book: The Wonderful World of Peaceful Worldschooling,[59] listen and learn through the Peaceful Worldschooling Podcast, and explore more about this new paradigm of education on my website: www.PeacefulWorldschoolers.com.

Friends, we are not without hope. We can begin to live and dream outside of this educational box that we have squeezed ourselves into for far too long. And while this book is coming to an end, I want you to know that the adventure is just beginning. I cannot wait to see what you and your children will create with the freedom that you are about to step into.

As you are creating an ideal educational environment for your child, I want you to ask yourself a few key questions. The first question is: **What do I want my child to learn?**

---

[59] https://peacefulworldschoolers.com/downloads/the-wonderful-world-of-peaceful-worldschooling/ This book is also available for purchase on Amazon.com.

One day, I got a phone call from a mother who could barely speak because she was holding back tears. Her daughter was just six years old and was continually being sent home from school for not wearing her mask properly. The mother was having issues at her work because she was repeatedly needing to leave early in order to pick up her daughter from school.

"I just can't do this anymore!" she cried. "I never wanted my daughter to wear a mask in school, and I cannot stand the thought of having her sitting on a computer for six hours a day for the virtual academy."

"Okay, it sounds like her schooling environment is not working very well for her or for you. Are there any other issues that your daughter has been experiencing?" I asked.

"My daughter has been having problems with bullies on her bus to the point that she misses the bus on purpose to avoid riding the bus with them. She didn't even tell me. I only found about it because some of the other parents at the bus stop mentioned that they had seen some of the bigger kids making fun of her and pushing her around."

"That's awful! I am so sorry that she is being bullied. I wish that I could say that her experience is the exception, but unfortunately, it's not. What did you do when you found out that she was being bullied?"

"I told the principal immediately, but she said that there is nothing that she can do. I asked her at what point do bullies lose the privilege of riding a bus to school, and the principal's response was: 'Well, we don't really do that because it would be an inconvenience for the students and their parents.' I almost lost my mind! So, it's okay for me and my daughter to be inconvenienced because of their bullying, but nothing happens to the actual bullies!"

We discussed the possibilities of removing her child from that toxic environment and creating a new, healthier educational environment for her. I asked her the same question that I asked you: "What do you want your child to learn?"

"Hmm... I suppose the basics. Reading and math."

Most of the time when I ask parents this question, they will respond with a similar answer. Parents are very concerned about their children learning reading and math, in particular. They will usually also rattle off some of the other core subjects like science and social studies.

"Now, I want you to answer that question again but, this time, pretend that school does not exist. What do you *really* want your child to learn?"

"Hmmm..." there was silence on the phone for a few seconds. She took a deep breath and said, "I have never thought about that before. I suppose, I would want my child to learn to be kind and to work hard."

"That's great!" I exclaimed. "When I asked myself this question a few years ago, I realized that what I *really* want my daughter to learn is exactly what you said. I want her to learn how to be kind, how to work hard, how to think critically, how to be creative, how to solve problems, how to have grit, how to stand up for what's right, how to be generous, how to help those in need, how to have empathy, how to be brave, how to be a good and faithful friend."

When we begin to think about the skills that make a person successful in life, you will find that those skills have less to do with a person's classes and more to do with a person's character. Any person can learn math or Spanish or piano, but the soft skills are the key to success in all areas of life.

The next question that I asked her was: **What are the life skills that you would want your child to learn?** I shared that I also wanted my daughter to learn some valuable life skills that I never learned when I was growing up like how to cook, how to clean, how to do laundry, how to grow your own food, how to start a business, and how to invest money.

Part of teaching life skills is also being aware of the skills that I can teach my child myself as well as the skills that I will need support with. I can teach my daughter how to cook some basic things, but because that was a skill that I did not have growing up, I signed both of us up for a mother-daughter cooking class so that we could both learn together.

While I believe that growing your own food is an important life skill, it is not one that I enjoy, so I asked one of my friends who is an avid gardener if she would be willing to have my daughter go to her house once a week so she could learn to grow different types of vegetables and herbs.

The final – and most important question – that we discussed was: **What does your *child* want to learn?** If you are not sure what you child wants to learn, then begin by asking: What does my child enjoy? Because we learn best that which we learn with joy.

My daughter loves to watch YouTube videos. Sometimes, I enjoy watching the videos with her, but there are times when she watches things on YouTube that really don't interest me at all – and that is okay. She is allowed to like different things that me.

One day, my daughter decided that she wanted to make her own YouTube channel. So, for Christmas, I bought her a camera with a video feature. We downloaded the app InShot so she could start to practice editing the videos that she was taking. One of my friends who is a YouTuber came over to teach her how to make and edit her own intro and outro. We watched countless YouTube videos about how to make YouTube videos. She learned how to create a channel, how to upload videos, how to write the titles and descriptions, how to edit the videos, how to add music, how to use time lapse and slow-motion features, how to add effects and transitions, and more!

I forgot to mention that my daughter is 7 years old.

There are adults that do not know how to do those things (myself included). And there are also adults that get paid a lot of money to do those things. But more than anything, I have enjoyed watching my daughter pursuing her passions and learning skills that are valuable for *her*.

When we can begin to lay aside our own agenda and to see our child as a unique individual with unique passions, gifts, interests, and talents that are uniquely theirs, then we can begin to create the ideal educational environment and experience for that child.

We, as parents, can find supplies, books, videos, classes, teachers, experts, resources, and more to support our children in learning the things that are most important to them. Learning does not have to be forced or coerced. It can truly be as simple as living and loving life together. If you give your child the gift of educational freedom, you will be amazed at what they will create.

Invite your child to be a part of the process of choosing what and when and how they learn. Invite your child to set their own goals and devise their own plan to reach those goals. Step back and watch your child take ownership of their life and their learning. Step in to offer assistance when and if they ask. Step down from your pedestal and become a student of your child. And step forward into the future of education – free, self-directed learning.

An educationally free, self-directed learner is a lifelong learner, and that is the goal of all true education – cultivating a love of learning for life. A self-directed learner is:

- **Self-Motivated:** eager to learn and to take responsibility for their own learning activities
- **Self-Managing:** controlling their own behaviors and resources required to optimize learning

- **Self-Monitoring:** thinking and evaluating their own learning goals and outcomes
- **Self-Modifying:** changing behaviors and processes based on self-monitoring and feedback received from others

If you are a Toxic Teacher and would like to inspire your students to be self-directed learners, I would encourage you to envision the kind of educational environment that you would like to create and the kind of teacher that you would like to be. Close your eyes and imagine the world of learning that you would like to see before you. Where are you? What are you doing? What are the students doing? How are you feeling? How are your students feeling? How are you all interacting with one another and with the world? With that image in your mind, take actions that are consistent with your vision for educational freedom.

There are infinite opportunities for teachers to contribute their knowledge and skills to the world outside of a traditional classroom, but one of the best ways that you can bring educational freedom to your students in or out of the classroom is through **ungrading**. Ungrading is literally eliminating all forms of grades, points, and scores from your classroom. Alfie Kohn writes that the three main effects of grading are that they reduce:

THE ANTIDOTE

1. Students' interest in the learning itself[60]
2. Students' preference for challenging tasks[61]
3. Students' quality of thinking[62]

Instead of grades, focus on providing students with authentic feedback and encourage your students to be self-directed learners by monitoring their own learning and evaluating themselves. Some other problems with grades are that grades:

1. Are not valid, reliable, or objective[63]
2. Distort the curriculum
3. Waste time that could be spent on learning
4. Encourage cheating[64]
5. Destroy teachers' relationships with students
6. Destroy students' relationships with each other[65]

---

[60] Kohn, A. *Punished by Rewards: The Trouble with Gold Stars, Incentive Plans, A's, Praise, and Other Bribes*. Boston: Houghton Mifflin, 1993
[61] Harter, S. "Pleasure Derived from Challenge and the Effects of Receiving Grades on Children's Difficulty Level Choices." *Child Development* 49 (1978): 788-99
[62] Butler, R. "Enhancing and Undermining Intrinsic Motivation: The Effects of Task-Involving and Ego-Involving Evaluation on Interest and Performance." *British Journal of Educational Psychology* 58 (1988): 1-14.
[63] Kirschenbaum, H., S. B. Simon, and R. W. Napier. *Wad-Ja-Get?: The Grading Game in American Education*. New York: Hart, 1971.
[64] Anderman, E. M., T. Griesinger, and G. Westerfield. "Motivation and Cheating During Early Adolescence." *Journal of Educational Psychology* 90 (1998): 84-93.
[65] Kohn, A. *No Contest: The Case Against Competition*. Rev. ed. Boston: Houghton Mifflin, 1992.

In addition to getting rid of grades, you can also get rid of all other requirements – including classwork and homework. In a learning environment where nothing is required, and everything is optional, students are free to learn what and how and when they want. Students are free to choose the assignments that they want to participate in or not based on the benefits of each assignment which you communicate to them in advance. In the words of Missouri teacher, Dorothy de Zouche, "If I can't give a child a better reason for studying than a grade on a report card, I ought to lock my desk and go home and stay there." She wrote those words in 1945, but their sentiment is just as true today.

For more information about ungrading, I encourage you to read Susan D. Blum's book, *Ungrading: Why Rating Students Undermines Learning (and What to Do Instead)* and Alfie Kohn's book *Punished By Rewards: The Trouble with Gold Stars, Incentive Plans, A's Praise, and other Bribes.*

I began this book by confessing that I am a Toxic Teacher. And I want to end this book by reminding us all of the antidote. The antidote to a Toxic Teacher is: *freedom*. Whether you are a parent or a teacher or both, be free – as you were meant to be. Resist tyranny and tyrants. Resist abuse and abusers. Resist slavery at all costs. This is the hill I will die on. And this is the hill I will live on. I will pave the way to freedom tomorrow with the choices that I make today. Will you join me?

THE CHAINS OF BEING CONFINED IN THE CLASSROOM HAVE MADE SLAVES OF US ALL.

— ANGELA HARDERS

CHAPTER 11
Epilogue

While Toxic Teachers have existed as long as schools have been invented, I personally had not seen the extent of the evil that came with the school system's systematic and systemic abuse of teachers and students until the COVID-19 crisis.

As I write this now, I am currently on administrative leave pending termination from my career as a teacher for "insubordination." How was I insubordinate, you may ask? I refused to wear a face covering – even though I have both medical and religious reasons for not wearing one.

You see, over the years I have grown adept at identifying and resisting abuse in the world because I am a survivor of abuse. At nineteen years old, I lost my virginity due to a violent rape in which an evil man took power and control over me. He covered my mouth and nose with one hand and choked me around my neck with his other hand. I struggled to breathe, and as he banged my head into the wall over and over and over again, I feared that I would die.

Ever since getting raped, I have been unable to have anything covering my mouth and my nose because it almost immediately causes me to have panic attacks and horrendous flash backs. In fact, I submitted medical exemption letters from two different medical providers to my school district that can attest to that fact.

I know that for many people, it may be "just a mask," but not for me. It is a reminder of abuse and violence. It is a symbol of submission and slavery. It is a mark of manipulation and malevolence. It is a cover up of compliance and coercion meant to cover us up and hide one of the most disastrous cover ups of all time. It's not "just a mask" for me.

And I am not alone. There are countless others that are just like me –survivors of rape and abuse – that can intuitively sense the scent of a psychopath. As survivors, we become acutely aware of the abuse that occurs around us which is why the response of abused people to this whole situation has become so visceral.

EPILOGUE

As my eyes began to be opened to the abuse that was not only happening right before my eyes, but that I was forced to take part in, I knew that I needed to break free. The thought of teaching to a sea of masked faces made me sick to my stomach. The idea that I would need to comply with force, coercion, manipulation, and threats against myself, my colleagues, and my students was utterly unbearable to me.

I was a Toxic Teacher, and I needed to be free. I *am* free. But freedom from a toxic system is not free. It has cost me greatly. My name has been slandered in the media and in the news. I have been defamed by colleagues and abandoned by people that I once called my friends. My fight for freedom is still not over as there are thousands more in my county and across the country that are about to lose their jobs over mask and vaccine mandates.

Regardless of your view on masks or vaccines, I want you to know that the issue itself is *not* the masks or the vaccines. The issue at hand is *freedom*. The issue at hand is choice. The issue at hand is the answer to a simple question: **Do human beings have a moral right to treat one another with force, threats, coercion, intimidation, manipulation, isolation, gaslighting, punishment, bribes, emotional abuse, financial abuse, and even physical abuse?** Your answer to that question makes all the difference in the world. And the actions that you take that reflect your integrity regarding this morality makes all the difference in the world.

This book is my attempt to answer this question as it relates to the field of education, but the question itself goes far beyond the world of education. It applies to every single area of life. My answer to that question may cost me my job and my career as a teacher. But it is worth it to lose a job if that means that I may cling tightly to my integrity and morality.

Since I have been placed on administrative leave without pay, I have been working diligently writing this book that I started so many years ago. Instead of trying to remain on board of a sinking ship, I am building a new one like Noah and the ark.

I created the PAX Ministries and the Center for Autodidact Services and Support (CASAS) as a way to provide families with educational freedom and inspire others to become Peaceful Worldschoolers like me and my family.

Peaceful Worldschoolers are committed to cultivating peace in the world beginning right in our own hearts and homes. We are committed to treating others with kindness, gentleness, love, patience, and respect. We are committed to having all of our relationships be free from force, threats, coercion, intimidation, manipulation, isolation, gaslighting, punishment, bribes, emotional abuse, financial abuse, physical abuse, and violence of any kind. We are committed to being free and inspiring others to be free.

This book is just the beginning, and I am excited to create something new with each of you. I invite you to join the Peaceful Worldschooling Community. Together, we can create a beautiful

EPILOGUE

future for our children and for ourselves. There is much work to be done, but it starts with us.

If you are interested in exploring educational freedom for you and your children, please reach out to me. I am more than happy to help you begin this journey and to walk alongside you as you step into a role of empowering your children to be all that they desire to be instead of seeking power over them. I am excited to see the incredible things that you and your children will create as you pursue your passions and a life of faith and freedom.

Website: www.peacefulworldschoolers.com
Instagram: @PeacefulWorldschooler
Facebook: www.facebook.com/PeacefulWorldschoolers
YouTube: www.youtube.com/c/PeacefulWorldschoolers
Podcast: https://anchor.fm/peaceful-worldschoolers
Email: peacefulworldschooler@gmail.com

SPECIAL THANKS

I want to say a special "Thank You" to my best friend and partner, Patty Hurtarte.

Thank you for believing in me and supporting me all these years.

Thank you for painting the posters for my first classroom.

Thank you for helping me grade hundreds of Spanish tests.

Thank you for supporting me and my students in Guatemala.

Thank you for always saying "Heck yes!" to my goals.

Thank you for listening as I shared countless "teacher stories."

Thank you for designing a "Truth Lover, Freedom Fighter" Tee.

Thank you for encouraging me to pursue mental/physical health.

Thank you for rescuing me from toxic and dangerous situations.

Thank you for inspiring me to trust God, my kids, and myself.

Thank you for caring for my children so I could write this book.

Thank you for contributing your works of art to my work of art.

Thank you for being brave enough to leave your career to pursue your passions.

There are not enough pages in any book
nor enough words in any language
that can adequately express my sincere love
and eternal gratitude to you and for you.

This is my commandment:
Love one another as I have loved you.
Greater love has no one than this:
to lay down one's life for one's friends.
John 15:12-13

The artwork at the end of each chapter was brilliantly and beautifully designed by Patty "AP" Hurtarte @HurtarteStudio. You can purchase original and print pieces for your home at www.atfive31am.com.

Appendix A
The Power and Control Wheel

Violence

Physical · Sexual · Emotional · Emotional · Physical · Sexual · Violence

Power and Control

Using Coercion and Threats
- Making and/or carrying out threats or punishment
- threatening loss of freedom
- threatening authority involvement/prison
- threatening fines
- manipulating
- bribing

Using Force and Intimidation
- Making children afraid by using mean looks, actions, gestures
- Smashing or throwing things
- Standing over children
- Yelling and screaming
- Confiscating things
- Forcing to do useless tasks
- Silencing

Using Emotional Abuse
- Humiliating children
- Making them feel like failures
- Withholding love and compassion
- Publicly shaming and embarrassing them
- Stonewalling or ignoring the student
- Making fun of a student/name calling

Using Isolation
- Controlling what they do, where they go, who they talk to, what they read, etc.
- Isolating from family, friends, the community or the rest of class
- Putting students in "time out" or detention
- Taking away recess or lunch

Denying, Minimizing, and Blaming
- Making light of abuse
- Blaming the students
- Not taking concerns seriously
- Denying the abuse is happening
- Shifting responsibility for abusive behaviors
- Gaslighting a students' experience

Using Children
- feeling in control
- using children for power
- using children to do tasks
- feeling better about yourself
- threatening to take children away
- using children to communicate with parents or others

Using Adult Privilege
- Treating children like servants or "lesser"
- Enforcing but not following the rules
- Preventing meaningful participation
- Denying rights and privileges
- Making all of the decisions
- Always being "right"
- Inflicting pain
- Bossing

Using Economic Abuse
- Preventing students from getting or keeping a job
- Controlling financial decisions
- Stealing or destroying their belongings
- Withholding access to money that belongs to the students

Made in the USA
Middletown, DE
24 June 2023